# REDISCOVERING GOD

# Rediscovering God

## And Why We Never Have to Look

*Zacharias Heyes*

Paulist Press
New York / Mahwah, NJ

Cover image © by Giovanni Triggiani / Dreamstime.com
Cover design by Tamian Wood
Book design by Lynn Else

Library of Congress Cataloging-in-Publication Data
Names: Heyes, Zacharias, 1971– author. | Dahm Robertson, Peter, editor, translator.
Title: Rediscovering God : and why we never have to look / Zacharias Heyes; translated by Peter Dahm Robertson.
Other titles: Gott wieder finden. English
Description: New York : Paulist Press, [2020] | Originally published in 2018 by Vier-Tuerme, as Gott wieder finden : und warum es gar nicht nötig ist, ihn zu suchen. | In English, translated from original German. | Summary: "In Rediscovering God, Fr. Zacharias Heyes invites us to walk a new path toward seeing God amid our everyday life"— Provided by publisher.
Identifiers: LCCN 2019029722 (print) | LCCN 2019029723 (ebook) | ISBN 9780809155187 (paperback) | ISBN 9781587688522 (ebook)
Subjects: LCSH: Presence of God—Biblical teaching. | Christian life—Catholic authors. | Spiritual life—Catholic Church.
Classification: LCC BV4503 .H4913 2020 (print) | LCC BV4503 (ebook) | DDC 248.4/82—dc23
LC record available at https://lccn.loc.gov/2019029722
LC ebook record available at https://lccn.loc.gov/2019029723

ISBN 978-0-8091-5518-7 (paperback)
ISBN 978-1-58768-852-2 (e-book)

Published by Paulist Press
997 Macarthur Boulevard
Mahwah, New Jersey 07430
www.paulistpress.com

Printed and bound in the
United States of America

# Contents

v

# Contents

# Preface

In November 2016, my home monastery of Münsterschwarzach celebrated the 1200th anniversary of its founding. As part of the festivities, for an entire year, Father Meinrad Dufner put on a commemorative exhibit in our abbey church. This wasn't a historical and chronological account of the monastery's 1,200 years. It was more a "modernization" and "bringing up-to-date" of the Christian faith as we practice it. The exhibit also made use of the apse, including the altar. There, to the left of the large figure of Jesus resurrected, Father Meinrad had let down a long rope ladder from the ceiling. We could easily interpret this as Jacob's Ladder or a "stairway to heaven," but what made it so special was the presentation and interpretation of this work of art. The ladder was wrapped in gold foil, the kind that most of us know from first aid kits in cars. This golden ladder shone so brightly that it was easily visible from the entrance to the church and immediately drew the attention of most visitors. Many had the impression that the ladder was a permanent fixture of the space. That was how organic and fitting with our faith history and life circumstances it seemed.

First of all, Jacob's Ladder is a reference to the founding father of Israel in the Old Testament. After Jacob deceives Isaac and steals the birthright and blessing of Esau, his elder brother, Esau, wants revenge, and so Jacob flees to Haran. On the way to Haran, Jacob sets up camp for the night and falls asleep on a stone. Here he dreams of a ladder beginning on the stone and ascending into heaven, with angels going up and down the ladder. Jacob is so moved by this that when he wakes up, he says, "Surely the LORD is in this place—and I did not know it!" (Gen 28:16). This makes him afraid and he says, "How awesome is this place! This is none other than the house of God, and this is the gate of heaven" (Gen 28:17).

He uses oil to anoint the stone he has slept on and sets it up as a pillar for a memorial. Jacob vows that if God will keep him alive and see him safely through his trouble, Jacob will return to this place and build a temple for the Lord. Jacob understands that this is a place of God's presence. God is present on earth, not just "above" in heaven.

I remember how, when Father Meinrad first walked me and my fellow monks through this exhibition, the ladder opened my eyes to my own faith in a whole new way. This was mostly because of what one of my colleagues said. He reflected that Christianity is a religion whose significant characteristic is that man doesn't have to exert constant effort in order to have access to God or perform certain acts for God to accept him. In other words, a Christian doesn't need to spend all their time worrying about how to ascend to heaven or how far they have already come on the "stairway to heaven." Instead, Christianity starts from the premise that the fundamental movement occurs from God to humanity. To stay in the metaphor: God has descended from heaven and has already been approaching human beings for eons.

The decisive moment is when God became human in Christ. Christians believe that in Jesus, God himself became a man. He was close to people, gave them the gift of his love and friendship, healed them, and raised them up. The people he encountered took away new hope, faith, and strength. In Christ's humanity, God encountered human beings. God wants to be tangibly close and present among people because he loves humanity.

The gold of the foil that Father Meinrad wrapped around the ladder makes a symbolic point, not just an aesthetic one. As an incredibly precious metal, it points out the incalculable value of human dignity—the dignity that every human being has as a creature of God's Creation. To God, a person is worth immeasurably more than gold. If we are trying to find God, we don't need to run around in "search mode." Instead, we should be in a state of inner readiness to be found by God and to encounter God in the midst of all those around us.

But many generations were shaped by a form of Christian teaching that told people how they had to be, the sorts of things that "a good Christian" either did or wouldn't do, because in that view God actually did not love you if you did one thing or forgot something else. Even today, many Christians carry with them the thought that Jesus had to die on the cross because God required a sacrifice before he would forgive. Human sin, the argument goes, had angered, offended, and hurt God, making such a sacrifice necessary.

In contrast, the idea that God has found man and continues to approach and reach out to humanity can take some of that pressure off. We can let ourselves be found. This is a liberating idea.

In this book, I invite you to walk a new path with me, a path toward rediscovering God in the middle of your everyday life. In the first section of the book, our journey begins with biblical figures and the experiences they have with God. These are key experiences. In Jesus, we can then see that God is not only close by, he is not only with humanity; he is in humanity, has become human, and is there for all of us to experience. The second section leads us on to the discovery of God within ourselves and each other, because Jesus shows us that if you want to find God, you have to look for humankind. The third section is concerned with the resulting challenges for the church. If God is right in the middle of our lives, in our everyday encounters, both with and within people, then that's exactly where the church should be. The church has to approach people and be with them. This has consequences for services and rituals, and for the shape the church takes today. It begs the question: Is the church the arbiter and manager of tradition, rite, and form, or does it respond to the conditions of our lives today? Will it become rigid and unmoving, or will it seek the living God with and within living people?

I wish you an exciting and surprising journey in the coming chapters!

# CHAPTER 1

||||||||||||||||||||||||||||||||||||||||||||||||||||||||||||||

# God Finds Humankind

## *Key Biblical Experiences*

## ADAM AND EVE

The first account of the Creation in the Old Testament Book of Genesis explains how God made humankind on the sixth day—in the image of God. That statement will always be the foundation of every individual human being's unique dignity. Like every other part of creation, human beings aren't just a "coincidence" or a whim of evolution. We come from the will of God. This story has led more fundamentalist streams, particularly in the United States, to take it literally and completely reject the theory of evolution. But there are also an increasing number of those within science who say that, despite all the chance and coincidence that played a part, all of creation must have some sense, deeper meaning, or plan behind it all. This is where evolutionary theory and biblical narrative meet. The biblical narrative isn't meant to give an exact chronological account of how the world came to be. It's meant to answer the question, What's the idea behind the Creation?

Although evolutionary science can explain or postulate how everything in the universe came into being and what happened when, the Bible answers our questions about why or what it's all for. The stories of the Creation, found in Genesis 1:1–2:3 and 2:4–25, reflect this question about the origin of the cosmos. They were written based on the common worldview when they originated, about 500 BC. So, of course there are some sentences in them that seem very strange to us today. For me, one of these is Yahweh's command that humankind is supposed to "have dominion" over all of creation. Another one is the idea that woman was made out of man, or more precisely from Adam's rib. When dealing with these stories, however, it's important to filter out and recognize what they are actually saying, or even more so, what the intention is behind what they are saying. Unfortunately, the idea of God's giving humankind "dominion" over all the earth was taken too literally for a long time. What it actually means is dealing with creation in a way that protects Earth's resources and serves everyone. It's much less about "dominion" in the sense of using the world for our purposes and much more about taking responsibility so that people, animals, and plants can all live well.

Most societies in the past were—and many today still are—organized so that women are more like servants for men than equal partners. That comes in part from the Creation account where God made the woman from the rib of the man (Gen 2:21–23). Yet the first account also says that God created humankind as man and woman (Gen 1:26–28). That's very clear. There's no distinction, just "and." Togetherness and mutuality. When my native Germany was recently deciding whether or not to allow civil marriage for gay and lesbian couples, bishops and politicians kept referring back to that biblical passage, claiming that marriage must be a lifelong union of a man and a woman, because God had created human beings as man and woman. When that text was written, that was certainly the normal form of union. But what the Bible actually says is that God created humankind "male and female." That sounds more like God gave creation and humanity male and female *qualities*, which make people different from one another and interdependent. That also touches on the lives of all people who no longer fit into the classical image of a relationship between a man and a woman: those who feel, live, and love homosexually; those who don't feel themselves as clearly being a man or a woman; and those who feel that the body they were born in doesn't match who they are. We need to think through these topics theologically, while considering all the psychological and scientific insights we have today. If Christianity, based on the first account of Creation, has so far seen men and women as always clearly male or female, with one always uniquely made for the other, then we need to take a new look at how to make biblical sense of these ideas.

The Catholic Church may respect people who aren't heterosexual, but it doesn't allow them to live out their lives, experience their love, and choose their own path. In this context, I don't think seeing man and woman as made exclusively for one another is the only correct interpretation of the Creation story. The crucial aspect in the biblical account of the creation of humankind is that God initiated a process whereby humankind lives on the earth in his image. As beings in the image of God, every person deserves to be honored and respected, regardless of race, culture, or nation, and regardless of sexual orientation. People are never completely independent or isolated, so every person should have a partner equal to them. In this partner, they can and should recognize God's grandeur and beauty. God made humankind and has put himself within us. Interestingly, God sometimes talks about himself in the plural: "Let us make humankind in our image" (Gen 1:26).

This is either meant to emphasize God's authority or to provide a clue to an old idea: Early Jewish thought held that Yahweh had a "wife" named Asherah, who was so prominent that King Manasseh erected a monument to her. Only when Israel's faith became increasingly monotheistic were the references to Asherah slowly removed. The Book of Hosea actually has God speaking a traditional Jewish statement of divorce, which may again reflect the transition to monotheism. The important point is that God himself is relationship. In the Christian faith, the Trinity reflects this profound concept, where God in himself is the relationship among the three divine persons of Father, Son, and Holy Spirit. If we want to seek God today, we need to be in relation to one another, to see God's image and thus God in each other.

# ABRAHAM

Abraham is a seminal figure in the Bible, but also in the history of religion. Even today, we remember him as the historical patriarch of Jews, Muslims, and Christians. His son Ishmael by the maid Hagar is seen as the ancestor of Muhammad, the founder of Islam. Isaac, the son of Abraham by his wife, Sarah, is the father of Jacob, whose twelve sons in turn founded the twelve tribes of Israel, and thus Judaism. The tribe of Israel provides the ancestry for Jesus, the foundation and founder of Christianity. Hence, Abraham is at the beginning of a long religious history of Muslims, Jews, and Christians, all of whom dedicated their lives to the God of Abraham. Today, approximately four billion people belong to one of the three Abrahamic world religions, making clear how great an impact these have today.

Born into a nomadic family in Ur, a city in Chaldea (present-day southern Iraq), Abraham was accustomed to life on the move, rather than to a sedentary life. He knew the desert and the steppes well. Because Chaldea was home to many Babylonians, Abraham came into contact with and was influenced by the Babylonian religion, though the Bible doesn't clearly describe his religious practice. Like the Greeks and the Romans, the Babylonians had a pantheon of many gods, with each god standing for something. Babylonian gods included Sīn, in charge of the path of the moon, and Ishtar, the goddess of war and love.

After his father died, Abram (as he is called until later in the story) hears God speak to him for the first time. God has no other name here but is referred to only as "God." He instructs Abraham:

> Go from your country and your kindred and your father's house to the land that I will show you. I will make of you a great nation, and I will bless you, and make your name great, so that you will be a blessing. I will bless those who bless you, and the one who curses you I will curse; and in you all the families of the earth shall be blessed. (Gen 12:1–3)

Often, when people today face life transitions or are setting out into something new, we quote this mission to Abram from God. It shows us a theme that keeps returning throughout the Bible: the conviction and affirmation that God finds people, speaks to them, and trusts them to set out into the unknown. This makes God a god of journey and of setting out. When I talk to people in my role as a counselor, I see clearly how that hasn't changed up to today. Again and again, God calls us to set out on internal and external journeys of change or transformation in our lives. Journeys happen and we need to face them.

God speaks to Abram and calls him to leave the land he knows and go somewhere unknown. In the same way, Abram is in the process of discovering this God who speaks to him. In whatever way Abram hears God—an inner voice, a light from beyond himself, or in some other way, it's clear that this encounter will change his life. At this point, Abram is seventy-five years old, an age in our time when many are enjoying their retirement. But now he sets out again, inspired by God. Abram ventures on this journey with his whole family, with all his servants and employees. His nephew Lot journeys with him as well, and both take all their possessions along with them. In today's terms, Abram would be a billionaire. He owns cattle, silver, and plenty of gold. But Lot is rich too, with many sheep, goats, cows, and other possessions. Because they don't want to settle in the same place to avoid rivalries, Abram and Lot go their separate ways. God then appears to Abram again, this time saying,

> Raise your eyes now, and look from the place where you are, northward and southward and eastward and westward; for all the land that you see I will give to you and to your offspring forever. I will make your offspring like the dust of the earth; so that if one can count the dust of the earth, your offspring also can be counted. Rise up, walk through the length and the breadth of the land, for I will give it to you. (Gen 13:14–17)

God is promising Abram an infinite number of descendants, as many as there is dust on the earth. I'm sure we aren't meant to take this biologically. It refers to the many faithful of the Abrahamic traditions. Here, too, God finds a person and gives a mission.

At first, God's promise goes unfulfilled. Abram suffers because his wife cannot bear any children. He has followed God's mission but remains childless. Yet again, God finds Abram and speaks to him:

> "Do not be afraid, Abram, I am your shield; your reward shall be very great." But Abram said, "O Lord God, what will you give me, for I continue childless, and the heir of my house is Eliezer of Damascus?" And Abram said, "You have given me no offspring, and so a slave born in my house is to be my heir." But the word of the Lord came to him, "This

man shall not be your heir; no one but your very own issue
shall be your heir." He brought him outside and said, "Look
toward heaven and count the stars, if you are able to count
them." Then he said to him, "So shall your descendants
be." (Gen 15:1–5)

This time, Abram believes God. He trusts that he will have descendants. Because God considers Abram's behavior just, he is a role model
of faith and trust. That includes his role as father of the three Abrahamic
religions. He laid the foundation for people today to trust in God
because God, for his part, has proven himself trustworthy, as the rest of
the story shows.

Being "just" in God's eyes means nothing more or less than being
accepted by God, standing upright before God, and understanding
oneself as loved by God. People are still grappling with the question of
what it means to be accepted by God, to be just in God's eyes, despite
our own weaknesses, mistakes, and faults—our "sins." This was also
one of Martin Luther's central questions. He nearly despaired from
feeling his own imperfection so keenly. He knew that our actions alone
can't make us just before God, because we will always keep doing
unjust things. He finally realized that if we trust God (faith doesn't
mean anything other than "trust"), we will be just. This means that
God wants human beings to come into contact with him. He seeks
an answer to his approach, his speaking with humanity. The God of
Abram is a God of relationships, who wants to be in close contact with
his creatures. That is why he keeps finding and approaching human
beings, rather than leaving them to their own devices and fates. The
words God says to Abram he addresses in turn to all humankind. In
Abram (who becomes Abraham), the father of faith, we can see a clear
invitation: Believe in God and trust him.

When God says that Abram is supposed to count all the stars in the
sky if he can, it's this kind of invitation—he will have infinitely many
descendants. But this also expresses the breadth and generosity of God.
Not only does God let him look at the expanse of the land to the north,
south, east, and west, he also refers to the unimaginable size of the sky
and the countless number of stars. If God, as the Bible says, created all
this, think about how generous he's being! When I consider the infinity
of space, I sometimes feel overwhelmingly alone and lost, because from
a cosmic point of view, humanity is like a needle in a haystack. But God

created all this vastness, and that same God speaks to humankind, and sees and accepts every human being—not generally and globally, but personally: "I have called you by name, you are mine" (Isa 43:1).

My deepest conviction is that this is true. God knows every person through and through. I'm allowed to believe that God has made me just as I am, and therefore, however I am is the way God wanted me to be. Jesus says the same thing using different words: "Even the hairs of your head are all counted" (Matt 10:30). God has a loving eye on the tiniest aspect of every human being.

In Abram's case, this is reflected in his being given a new name before God. Once God's mission is clear to him and he has put his trust in God, his original name of "Abram" becomes "Abraham":

> When Abram was ninety-nine years old, the LORD appeared to Abram, and said to him, "I am God Almighty; walk before me, and be blameless. And I will make my covenant between me and you, and will make you exceedingly numerous." Then Abram fell on his face; and God said to him, "As for me, this is my covenant with you: You shall be the ancestor of a multitude of nations. No longer shall your name be Abram, but your name shall be Abraham; for I have made you the ancestor of a multitude of nations. I will make you exceedingly fruitful; and I will make nations of you, and kings shall come from you. I will establish my covenant between me and you, and your offspring after you throughout their generations, for an everlasting covenant, to be God to you and to your offspring after you." (Gen 17:1–7)

This is a covenant between Abraham and God. Abraham is now ninety-nine years old, but this number is probably meant more symbolically than as a real age. Ninety-nine is a single step, one year, away from one hundred. One hundred suggests a full life, and Abraham is on the threshold of this when God makes a covenant with him. Abraham agrees to the covenant by following God. Once a person has been found by God, has agreed to let her- or himself be found by God, and addressed by God, then that person is given to know that God's loyalty is unbreakable.

After the covenant, Yahweh grants Abraham the gift that gives Abraham the greatest joy when Abraham becomes father to a son. This time, too, God finds Abraham, coming to him in the form of three men who visit:

> The LORD appeared to Abraham by the oaks of Mamre, as he sat at the entrance of his tent in the heat of the day. He looked up and saw three men standing near him. When he saw them, he ran from the tent entrance to meet them, and bowed down to the ground. He said, "My lord, if I find favor with you, do not pass by your servant. Let a little water be brought, and wash your feet, and rest yourselves under the tree. Let me bring a little bread, that you may refresh yourselves, and after that you may pass on—since you have come to your servant." So they said, "Do as you have said." And Abraham hastened into the tent to Sarah, and said, "Make ready quickly three measures of choice flour, knead it, and make cakes." Abraham ran to the herd, and took a calf, tender and good, and gave it to the servant, who hastened to prepare it. Then he took curds and milk and the calf that he had prepared and set it before them; and he stood by them under the tree while they ate.
>
> They said to him, "Where is your wife Sarah?" And he said, "There, in the tent." Then one said, "I will surely return to you in due season, and your wife Sarah shall have a son." And Sarah was listening at the tent entrance behind him. Now Abraham and Sarah were old, advanced in age; it had ceased to be with Sarah after the manner of women. So Sarah laughed to herself, saying, "After I have grown old, and my husband is old, shall I have pleasure?" The LORD said to Abraham, "Why did Sarah laugh, and say, 'Shall I indeed bear a child, now that I am old?' Is anything too wonderful for the LORD? At the set time I will return to you, in due season, and Sarah shall have a son." (Gen 18:1–14)

Abraham and Sarah have a son, and they call him Isaac. For a man in Abraham's time, a son was crucially important. He was the continuation of the patriarchal line, the one who would manage and inherit the father's legacy, not just materially, but also in a spiritual sense. A father would pass on his faith and trust in God. A father would tell his son what kinds of experiences he had had with God, and that God is loyal and worthy of all trust.

Keeping with the symbolism of numbers, Abraham becomes a father at the age of one hundred. One is symbolic of God's generative power—the ability to bring increase. The multiplication of one by one hundred then stands for the fullness of God's creative power, especially to bring forth life. Therefore, in the birth of his son, Abraham experiences the full force of God's creative power. But this also gives Abraham the responsibility to pass on his trust in God to his son, who is his legitimate heir.

Abraham's trust in God is profoundly tested one more time, when God commands Abraham to sacrifice Isaac, Abraham's only son and heir. Abraham overcomes his resistance and starts to make the sacrifice, but an angel stops him at the very last moment, as described in Genesis 22. To this day, many people wonder what this story means. Can it really mean that God wants human sacrifice? Or is the important thing that an angel appears and stops Abraham? Or is Abraham suffering from a delusion, having confused the real God with what is his own image of God? In this reading, the story becomes another case where God decisively approaches Abraham, in the form of an angel. Abraham is found by God again, so that he can feel how God really is—God needs no sacrifices. What Abraham already knew deep down, he now sees clearly: God is great and generous, approaches human beings, knows their names, and needs no sacrifice to accept them.

In the history of religion, the time of Abraham is linked with the time when other archaic cults and religions stopped sacrificing human beings. In that context, the story makes it clear that the Israelites' God doesn't need sacrifices, and certainly not human sacrifice. That would be self-contradictory, too, as God first creates a human being, gives them life, and then demands it back. A true gift only happens when something is given freely, without expectation of getting something in return. God gives the gift of life because he loves. What kind of a God would he be if he gave life but then constantly demanded gratitude, made human beings feel indebted, or even demanded the return of the life he gave?

At the end of Abraham's story, the Bible says, "This is the length of Abraham's life, one hundred seventy-five years. Abraham breathed his last and died in a good old age, an old man and full of years, and was gathered to his people" (Gen 25:7–8).

I love the phrase "full of years." Abraham has had his fill of life, but he isn't sick of it. His age of 175 represents complete satisfaction with life. Abraham has tasted life. He has experienced, felt, and lived all its ups and downs. He has trusted in his God. He has let God find him and has found God again and again, and his God who went with him has never left him.

At the beginning of his mission, Abraham learned from God that he would be a blessing, and that came true. He became fruitful by fathering Isaac and Ishmael. Even today, the religions that originated with these two biblical figures look back to Abraham's faith, his trust in God. If he's a forebearer, then what's true of him is true of all his descendants: We are already found. Looking for God and questioning him is much less important than just becoming conscious of the fact that he is here. Today, many people still look for God "up there," in the heavenly spheres, in large, unusual events instead of in the everyday moments. However, letting ourselves be found and approached by God means seeing him in the everyday and understanding that he is here. He is wherever human beings are. The greatness of the sky, the infinity of stars and cosmos, tell us that God is as great, infinite, wide, and all-encompassing as the sky and stars, but he is also the one who calls each of us by our name, who approaches and speaks to us.

Christians often quote the sentence that God says to Abraham: "You will be a blessing." That's a big promise. It means that human beings are allowed and even meant to pass on something of God's blessing. We're supposed to tell others. Human beings are supposed to sense and experience God's presence—God's greatness and nearness—in other human beings.

# MOSES

The name Moses, loosely translated as "the one who was drawn out of the water," describes the way Moses's life starts out. Moses is born to an Israelite woman. At the time, the Israelites are enslaved in Egypt, and since the Egyptian pharaoh fears that the Israelites might gain too much power and rebel, he has all male heirs killed. When the child is three months old, Moses's mother puts him in a reed basket and lets the basket drift out onto the Nile River. Miriam, Moses's older sister, watches as the pharaoh's daughter, who has come to the river to bathe, pulls the basket out of the Nile, saving Moses. Although the daughter of the pharaoh sees that the child must be an Israelite, she takes him in as her own. Miriam suggests that she will get an Israelite to nurse and raise the child. Pharaoh's daughter agrees, and Miriam brings the baby's own mother to nurse him. Moses isn't just miraculously saved but can even grow up being cared for by his own mother. When Moses is older, his mother returns him to the court, and the pharaoh's daughter takes him as her own son. This chain of events already shows how deeply God cares for Moses by saving him, "drawing him out of the water," and giving him a future.

One day after Moses has become a young man, he wants to check up on his people and see how they're doing. While investigating, he witnesses a fight between an Egyptian and an Israelite, one of his own people. He beats the Egyptian to death and then flees to Midian, where he finds a new home and makes a family, growing old there. When he is over eighty years old and herding his father-in-law's sheep, one day, he goes "beyond the wilderness" (Exod 3:1), meaning he crosses the boundary of the area laid out for him to live within. Finally, he reaches Mount Horeb, and here, God appears to him in a burning bush—not in the glorious temple in Jerusalem, considered the dwelling place of God, not in some special grove, but in a simple, thorny bush in which fire signifies a divine encounter. This changes Moses deeply. God calls himself "I am who I am," telling Moses, "The place on which you are standing is holy ground" (Exod 3:5). In other words, "Where you're standing right now is a place where the Sacred is present. It's a place where I, God, am." That also makes clear that there is nowhere in the world where God is *not* present, no place where we can't find God.

Moses wasn't expecting this kind of encounter with God at all, least of all during his daily work. The mission God gives then sends him out of his everyday routine and gives him the great responsibility of leading the people of Israel out of slavery into freedom. It's only natural for Moses to doubt at first, as he wonders whether he can do this thing. In the end, Moses becomes certain that God is with him and finds the courage to set out. Moses, too, lets himself be found. He lets himself be approached by God and accepts God's mission.

# DAVID

The story of King David is a typical "surprised by God" story. Pope Francis often says that we all should be prepared to let ourselves be surprised by God—every day. In the story of David, the main subject is the selection of a new king. The prophet Samuel is sent to Jesse the Bethlehemite because one of Jesse's eight sons will become the new king. After Samuel has seen the first seven sons, and none appears as the king chosen by God, Samuel asks about the eighth son. Jesse answers that David is working, guarding the sheep. But Samuel insists that he be summoned, too.

Number symbolism is important in this story. The number seven stands for the Creation, since God's work of creating the Earth and all it contains lasted seven days. Our week has seven days. Eight goes beyond seven and is therefore the number of perfection or eternity. This already seems to show that Jesse's eighth and youngest son is going to be special.

When David is called before Samuel, the prophet realizes that this is the new king chosen by God. Then Samuel anoints David king, pouring a horn of precious oil over his head. Being anointed with special and precious oil is a sign of being chosen and given special dignity, which marks David as the king of Israel. David, the simple shepherd, can feel his significance to God in his very body. How must he have felt when God suddenly stepped into his life, when God found him? He couldn't predict the enormous responsibility he would have to carry because of it.

David's anointment as king has echoes in today's rite of baptism, specifically in the chrismation, when the priest anoints the head of the baptized person with chrism, a consecrated oil. It reminds us of the anointment of the kings of Israel, and thus of the anointment of David. It expresses the royal dignity that God gives us. Every person who is baptized has dignity that no one can take away. God affirms each as a beloved child. Of course, every other person is God's beloved child too, but in baptism this affirmation is given publicly, before the parents and godparents as a witness.

Faith has always had a lot to do with the senses and with sensual experience. Today, many different baptism rites exist only in an abbreviated form. Immersion of one's naked body in water, which the early church practiced, has turned into three drops of water, carefully dripped over the baptized person. The sensual anointment with precious oil has turned into a cross made on the forehead. Yet we must make the feeling of being found by God experiential and tangible, so that it puts down roots in the soul as an unshakable certainty. That is what I would want to bring back to how we practice baptism today. What if rather than a few drops of water being poured over the head, a noticeable amount of water was used? Wouldn't it be clearer if the whole head were anointed with oil, and not just the sign of the cross being made with oil on the forehead?

# MARY

Mary was a simple girl of Israel. When the Bible picks up her story, she is about fourteen years old. She can't have imagined that she will become the mother of God, much less have pictured the huge importance that her story and her memory will have over the centuries. She is engaged to Joseph. He's often portrayed as an older man, although the Bible doesn't give any reason for doing so.

In the middle of her everyday chores, Mary is surprised by an angel who tells her that she will bear a son. According to the biblical record, it's the angel who starts the conversation. Because Mary isn't just surprised, but also scared, the angel starts off by saying, "Do not be afraid" (Luke 1:30). This is God's pedagogy. If God has entrusted a task to someone and informs them by angelic messenger, he doesn't want the listener to be afraid.

Mary answers when the angel talks to her. She asks how she will become a mother. The angel answers that the Holy Spirit will come over her, and Mary agrees. She simply submits to God's will. She has enough trust that she is willing to let this happen, even though she knows the social problems this will bring, and what she is asking of Joseph. Just as Mary trusts in God and in the fact that all will be fine if she follows God, we can also trust in the things God has planned for us. The Bible later says, "Mary treasured all these words and pondered them in her heart" (Luke 2:19). She needs to process this encounter, needs time to really understand what has happened, that she has been in direct contact with a divine messenger. God found her.

# JOSEPH

Joseph is, as we would say today, a man of integrity. When he hears about Mary's pregnancy, he wants to break up with her to save her the disgrace she would face if someone found out that the child isn't his. But God speaks to him in a dream, saying, "Joseph, son of David, do not be afraid to take Mary as your wife, for the child conceived in her is from the Holy Spirit" (Matt 1:20).

There is a beautiful saying: Dreams are God's forgotten language for speaking with us human beings. When we sleep, our conscious mind is "turned off." We can't set up any "filters" or go into denial or repress anything. That's why dreams are a wonderful possibility for God to communicate with the dreamer. Spiritually, the point of dreams is to make people see what processes are going on in their life and soul. To put it differently, dreams show what things want to happen and what that person must do. The goal is always that the dreamer walks his or her life's path. For that, God finds the person in a dream and communicates indirectly.

Joseph immediately accepts the mission he is given in his dream. He has faith, he trusts, so he lets God approach and speak to him. He doesn't question what God is telling him. As human beings who seek to understand God's daily dialogue with us, we need to open sensitive channels within us, to take dreams seriously and try to understand them.

When Francis became pope, he spoke about Joseph and his capacity for tenderness. The new pope told us that Joseph is not only brave, strong, and hardworking, but tender as well. He is ready to pay attention, have empathy, and be open to others. That's why he can hear God's message and understand it. That's also how he can take Mary to himself and to care for her and Jesus. Pope Francis talks about Joseph as a caregiver. He cared for his family and for his own soul. In order to hear God speaking to us, we need this tender, caring openness in our soul. Today, that's more important than ever, because our world is often so loud, and many things distract us from our inner life. One important goal can be to sharpen our sense for the language of our soul and of God with us. Joseph receives other important messages in dreams, too, about going to Egypt to save young Jesus's life, and returning because Herod has died.

# ZACCHAEUS

Zacchaeus was a tax collector. At the time, this profession was even more unpopular than it is today. Tax collectors back then took too much money from traders or others who had to cross city walls, a bridge, or some other border. Zacchaeus has made a little fortune by doing this. When he hears that Jesus is coming to Jericho, he wants to see him. We don't know what causes this wish in Zacchaeus. Has he heard about Jesus, about the loving way Jesus encountered others? Does he feel a deep longing to receive even just one loving glance from Jesus because no one else loves or even likes him?

Because Zacchaeus is short and worries that Jesus will overlook him or the crowd will push him aside, he climbs up a tree. When Jesus comes to where Zacchaeus is sitting in the tree, something unexpected happens. Jesus gives Zacchaeus much more than a loving glance. He sees Zacchaeus, calls him down from the tree, and tells him that the two will eat together. Jesus invites himself over to Zacchaeus's house. We can imagine that this self-invitation would have caused surprise, even outrage in some of the people around them. Here is this famous healer, whom some are even calling the Messiah, visiting the city, and then he goes and stays with a man who everyone knows is dishonest.

Today, we can see a parallel to this story in Pope Francis's encounters with people on fences or on the street, and in his Friday surprise visits, where he shows up unexpectedly and unannounced to visit people who are sick. The pope did something surprising during Holy Week of 2013 when he read the Holy Thursday liturgy not in the Vatican, but in a prison, even washing the feet of Muslim inmates! Pope Francis showed them that he sees them, knows their troubles, just as Jesus did with Zacchaeus two thousand years ago. For Zacchaeus, this visit sparks an unexpected change. When Jesus is at home with him, he decides to give back all the money he has wrongfully taken from people—even to return it double. On top of that, he wants to give away half his fortune.

So often, people think they need to be "without sin" or even "holy" to find God. But this story shows us the opposite path. God finds people and shows himself in his son, Jesus, in whatever situation people happen to be. He doesn't expect moral perfection. He gives loving acceptance and merciful closeness. He finds Zacchaeus and invites

15

himself into Zacchaeus's home. I'm fascinated by the words Jesus uses, when he says, "Zacchaeus, hurry and come down; for I must stay at your house today" (Luke 19:5).

It's as if Jesus has no other choice. He feels an urge to extend acceptance. It seems that part of his nature, his character, is to show and offer his own presence (meaning God's presence) to people who are on the margins. That can become the moment when a person changes. It can be a fresh start because that person experiences the unconditional love and acceptance for which they are most longing. It's the feeling that you're fine just the way you are.

# THE SAMARITAN WOMAN AT JACOB'S WELL

In this Bible story, Jesus is resting at Jacob's Well in Samaria when a Samaritan woman comes to fetch water. Jesus speaks to her and asks her for some water. At the time, this was a cultural and religious taboo for Jesus to appeal not only to a woman for a drink, but to a Samaritan woman, who was an outcast even to her own people! To the Jews of the time, and therefore to Jesus as well, Samaritans were heathens. They had their gods, but they didn't worship the Jewish God, Yahweh, or at least didn't worship him exclusively. Jesus deliberately seeks contact with such a woman; he actually approaches and addresses her.

In the course of their conversation, the woman asks Jesus about faith. Some say that one can pray to God only in the temple in Jerusalem, but her fathers have also prayed to God on Mount Gerizim, at the foot of which she and Jesus are standing. Which is true? Jesus answers her that God is spirit and people pray to God in the spirit. In that way, he is positioning himself, and clearly articulating his view that God isn't bound to one place. Elsewhere, Jesus says that the Spirit of God blows where he will. God is not geographically fixed. People can find him and let themselves be found by him wherever they happen to be. He cannot be pinned down or dogmatically cornered. These views make Jesus revolutionary for his time. And this revolution runs through all his statements. He is expanding the idea of God, which so far Jewish belief linked to encountering God's presence in the temple in Jerusalem. Jesus keeps emphasizing that God can't be pinned down.

God isn't subject to human demands, but if a person wants to seek or find him, they will find him everywhere — in the temple just as much as anywhere else.

# JESUS'S DISCIPLES

The people Jesus called to go with him and follow after him were all simple craftsmen or fishermen. Today, looking at the requirements for people who see following Jesus as their calling and want to become priests, I don't think the disciples would stand a chance. As fishermen, they knew the waters and where and when they would be able to catch fish. That was how they supported their families. When Jesus started preaching publicly, he was traveling around the villages and towns on the Sea of Galilee.

It's interesting that all his disciples, we're told, drop everything at once and go with him when Jesus calls them to follow after him. What causes them to follow a strange young man they have never seen before? Is it his charisma, clarity of his words, or a rumor that here is a remarkable human being, a person who teaches like someone with divine power?

So they are called straight out of their everyday lives, because that's right where Jesus finds them and speaks to them. Again and again, he surprises people. He invites them just the way they are. He brings them into contact with a different dimension of their lives. They will feel that he has something to offer or to tell them that they have never seen or heard anywhere else before, maybe even something they didn't know they were looking for.

Many other people, however, are traveling with Jesus aside from his twelve disciples. Another Bible passage describes how he sends out seventy-two disciples. These seventy-two go out in pairs, so that none of them is alone on the path. They are supposed to give one another strength. When one of them has lost track of God's presence, or is depressed, listless, or feels rejected because people turn him out instead of joyfully accepting him, in those moments, the other can encourage, strengthen, and help him, and clear his head. Jesus says, "For where two or three are gathered in my name, I am there among them" (Matt 18:20).

No one is supposed to feel alone and left behind. God shows himself particularly in the presence of another person who encourages and strengthens. In one of his audiences, Pope Francis said, "[Jesus Christ] does not accept that the human being exhausts his entire existence with this indelible 'tattoo,' with the thought of not being able to be welcomed by the merciful heart of God."[1] This experience of feeling loved and welcomed is incredibly important. It's easiest to feel this love of God through somebody else because then we can feel it in the body.

The Bible also talks about women who walked with and supported Jesus. One of them is Mary Magdalene, who in Catholicism has the official title of *apostola apostolorum,* or apostle of the apostles. Jesus's disciples, who walked with him during his life and traveled with him through Galilee to Jerusalem, are all known as "apostles" because they encountered the resurrected Jesus and were sent by God to proclaim his resurrection. But Mary Magdalene was the first person to encounter Jesus after his resurrection. The Bible says seven demons were exorcised from her. At the time, people understood a demon as some power that limited a person's life force. We should assume that Jesus healed Mary Magdalene, that he returned her to her full life force, and that she then went with him. This makes her one of the people whom Jesus found. She let herself be approached by Jesus.

On the morning of Easter, after his death, Jesus again addresses Mary Magdalene. He finds her. This time she really is looking for him, for his body, in order to anoint it with oil, as was the custom at the time. But when she looks into the tomb, it's empty. She then speaks with a man she thinks is the gardener and asks him where he has taken Jesus. She doesn't recognize the person as Jesus until he calls her by her name. When Jesus says, "Mary!" her eyes are opened. There must be a unique sound to how Jesus says her name, a sound filled with his love and acceptance of her, because she immediately recognizes him, turns to him, and calls him "Rabbouni," that is, Teacher. Mary Magdalene recognizes Jesus by his voice. She finds the one she was looking for and whom her soul loves.

From this encounter, and from the knowledge that the man she believed dead is alive, she gains the courage and strength to go and spread the news that Jesus rose from the dead. It's an important honor that she is called "apostle of the apostles," even today. Jesus's twelve disciples hid when Jesus was being nailed to the cross. The women didn't look away. The Gospel of John says that "standing near the cross of Jesus were his mother, and his mother's sister, Mary the wife of Clopas, and Mary Magdalene" (John 19:25). They stayed with the man who had found and addressed them, who had invited them to walk beside and stay with him. They could feel a sense of who this Jesus is, and that feeling was more powerful than fear.

After the resurrection, the disciples, too, are once again found and sent on a mission. What all these disciples share is that without debate, doubt, or questioning—they followed Jesus and his teaching after he found them. They also share a desire to bring their experiences with God and Jesus into the world. They do this consistently and until the very end, even if they may have to die for their faith and experience of having been found by God.

# JESUS

A completely different culture than that of Europe and the West shaped Israel, where Jesus grew up. I realized this when I started looking more closely at Jesus's native language, Aramaic. It's a language full of imagery and poetry, and every sentence, even every word, can have multiple meanings. Neil Douglas-Klotz, an American theologian, has studied Aramaic for many decades, especially Jesus's most well-known prayer, which we often call "The Lord's Prayer." He based his research on an Aramaic version of the New Testament from the second century, which is closest to the text that Jesus prayed and taught his disciples. Here, I will only discuss the opening lines. In our current version, the prayer begins with the words "Our Father, who art in heaven."

In one of his sermons, Pope Francis pointed out that the great revolution of Christianity is that God is a father, instead of somebody to fear. God is nothing but loving acceptance. Pope Francis called the central act of Christian prayer "the courage to call God by the name of Father." This means exactly that tender closeness between God and humanity, which is like the tender closeness between a father and child. Sure, the fact that we tend to address God as father rather than mother is due to the patriarchal worldview in which monotheism developed. But God is also Mother, and we must not one-sidedly define God by male attributes. We see this most clearly by looking at the original form of the Lord's Prayer.

The Aramaic prayer begins with the word *abwun*, which is gender-neutral, meaning father and mother, but also much more than parent. A literal translation might be: "O child-bearer! Father-mother of the cosmos." This sees God as a great unity of mother and father, a child-bearer from whom the cosmos springs, out of whom the Creation is born. Out of her and him, strength and blessing flow into the Creation, into the cosmos. Through this force, the Creation and the child-bearer are united. Jesus himself conceives of the cosmos as One, sees all life and every living thing as connected to its origin in God.

Although many people today think of heaven and earth as two different "geographic locations," Jesus's thinking is shaped by the idea of unity, that everyone and everything is connected to its divine origin in every moment. In Jesus's understanding, heaven does not mean a heaven "above"—the way we look at the sky. Instead, heaven is a different way of talking about God and his presence. Heaven is the great unity from which all human beings came in the beginning, from which we entered into our earthly life.

Just like the Judeo-Christian story of the Fall from Grace, many other religions have origin or Creation stories in which humanity goes from a state of divine unity into duality. Humanity's greatest longing is to return to this unity, to never again have to experience division or separation. It is about returning to one's original unity with God.

For a long time, the church was constantly making people aware of their own sinfulness, often in an attempt to keep people small. But what sin actually means is separation, being cut off. It means that there are situations where a person can't feel their connection to God, where they can't feel it because they have fallen into fear that God might not love them or that they are unlovable, because they can't find a way out of their own patterns and blockages. But God doesn't cut himself off from a human being. He doesn't draw away. God is always present in the world, God's Creation, and in human beings. We need to get back to an awareness that we are one with God, or to the insight that there's nothing that can truly separate us from God. That's why we don't need to look for God—he was never hidden and never hiding. He wants to be found, to be rediscovered. He never stops knocking on our human doors, making himself known and courting us in order to be in a relationship with us. There is a passage in the Gospels that makes this clear, when Jesus says, "But whenever you pray, go into your room and shut the door and pray to your Father who is in secret; and your Father who sees in secret will reward you" (Matt 6:6).

It's possible to read this sentence moralistically, as a diatribe against hypocrites who like to show themselves off and be seen. But on the poetic level of the Aramaic language, this sentence can also mean "Go into the room of your heart." In other words, "Go inside yourself, into the space where the father-mother-God is waiting for you." This is another sign that God has found a person—he is present inside them. Jesus makes the same point in a different way when he appears to his disciples after his death and resurrection. He sends the disciples out to spread his good news, and he breathes on them and says, "Receive the Holy Spirit" (John 20:22).

God's Spirit is mentioned at the very beginning of the Creation. It's the force that orders and molds chaos into shape and form. This Spirit acts in the entire cosmos, and thus in human beings as well. Jesus passes it on so clearly in this moment, breathing his own breath into the disciples, literally "inspiring" them so that they can pass on his Spirit and spread his good news to all those who hear.

In the story of Pentecost, there's another image of how the disciples are filled with God's Spirit, as tongues of flame settle above each of them (Acts 2:1–4). This image suggests that the Divine Spirit wanted to inflame them, to make them fiery. In fact, Jesus's disciples do find the courage to go out into the world and talk about God and Jesus.

The word *abwun* that I mentioned earlier can have another meaning as well: "O You, breathing life into everything!" This means that God is not only close to people, seeking them out and finding them in their specific everyday lives, but is actually a force that lives and breathes within them. God's Spirit, and therefore God himself, lives and is alive in each of us. In our breath, God breathes in us.

# Notes

1. Pope Francis, *General Audience*, August 9, 2017, Vatican Publishing Library, http://w2.vatican.va/content/francesco/en/audiences/2017/documents/papa-francesco_20170809_udienza-generale.html.

# CHAPTER 2

||||||||||||||||||||||||||||||||||||||||||||||||||||||||||||

# Discovering God

## *Do Not Seek. Find!*

I once read an interesting quote from Pablo Picasso: "I do not seek. I find." It's easy to wonder whether that's the same thing. If someone is seeking, don't they want to find? To me, this Picasso quote is all about point of view. Many people put a lot of energy into looking for things. Some even look for things their whole life and never find them. They never arrive and are never satisfied. But a person who travels through life with the inner thought "I'm finding things!" will be willing to arrive, to find. They'll be willing to see: "This is what I've been looking for."

It reminds me a little bit of a sentence that was "hip" for a while: "It's the journey that matters, not the destination." That's true, but how can you worry about your journey without having some goal of where you want to go? We need to honor our path, no question, and all the important experiences we gain along the way. Without the things I lived through on my pilgrimage to Santiago de Compostela, I wouldn't be the person I am today. Again and again in life, you need to set out, go on a journey, and say goodbye to paths that can't support you anymore. But it's also about finding, about arriving anew. In the context of God, that can mean letting go of old, hardened ideas about what God is like, or how I want him to be.

People in the Old Testament were surprised when they encountered God, but more importantly, people who came into contact with

Jesus were surprised. They all had in common that they encountered God in places where they didn't expect him, and maybe also that they weren't looking for God at all, but he found them. Often, though, we look for God in the places where we expect to find him, such as in churches, sermons, holy sites, or on pilgrimages. That means we lose sight of the fact that, even these days, God encounters us where we don't expect him, or even more so, where we have stopped looking and just let ourselves be found by him. God encounters us where we set out with an attitude of "I'm not seeking; I'm finding!" In the following chapters, I'll take a closer look at some of the places where we can find God.

# FINDING GOD WITHIN ME

## Humankind as the Image of God

Recently, I've been having a lot of discussions about the question of whether God is male or female, or whether God can even be put into these categories, since he's always above and beyond, always greater than human categories. When I read the Bible passage that says humankind is made in the image or likeness of God, and that humankind is male and female, then to me that means, first of all, that God has both male and female qualities. In the context of humankind being made in the image of God, modern psychology has more fundamentally expressed God's male and female nature in the insight that every person carries both male and female aspects within them. In growing up, every person must find a way of letting both aspects live in her- or himself, and of integrating both into his or her personality. Psychoanalysis refers to the male side of a person as the *animus* and the female side as the *anima*.

Christians believe that God became human in Jesus Christ, and Jesus says, "Whoever has seen me has seen the Father" (John 14:9). But this doesn't mean that Jesus is referring to his being male! That Jesus was male doesn't let us conclude that God is only male, even if that's how he was presented over years. That's not to mention that most pictures show him as a kindly, white-bearded grandfather rather than as a strict, clear-eyed judge or a fit young man with rock-hard abs.

Jesus's statement about himself has more to do with his inner character and his actions toward others than with his outward appearance. In Jesus, we can see *how* God is. His actions let us read how God acts toward humankind. All the images Jesus uses speak to how God lives in and encounters people. For example, Jesus talks about God as a loving father who welcomes back the son who has squandered his fortune. He talks about God as a shepherd who cares for every single sheep, and that's exactly how Jesus acts. Whenever he encounters people, his attitude is always kind. He looks with a loving, forgiving, and caring eye. Sometimes he looks with sadness, when he feels pain that someone who wants to follow him feels they can't. When he finds his friend Lazarus dead, he is shaken to the bone. In Jesus, God shows himself as compassionate, letting himself be touched by the suffering and hardship of people around him. He shows himself as the one who freely gives loving attention to all people, who raises them up, and encourages and heals them. But he is also just as much a decisive, clear, and challenging figure. In the Gospels, Jesus often says, "Get up!"

In those words we find his unequivocal will for another person to rise with strength to walk their own path. If humankind is made in the image of God, then each person can reveal God's nature. That means that all of us can address others lovingly with both our male and female aspects to raise others up. We can strengthen and encourage them to get up and walk their path. That is still the foundation of humankind's unique dignity. Because humankind is made in God's image and is uniquely shaped by God, humankind is also infinitely valued by God.

When we understand ourselves as made in God's image, we can find God's different aspects revealed in our abilities and skills, which are revealed in both male and female traits. But being made in God's image isn't just about looking inside ourselves. We can see God's creativity, multidimensionality, and grandeur in external beauty, in the incredibly varied image looking back at us from billions of faces in the world, each one uniquely and individually made.

# Humankind as a Space for God

In 2017, our abbey held a Pentecost symposium titled "Bridges to God," presenting many different paths to God from within the traditions of Christianity, Islam, and Judaism. These three Abrahamic religions share a belief in one God, although they give him different names. While Jews see God's name as holy, and saying it is taboo, Christians call him God or Jehovah ("I am here"), and Muslims call him Allah.

At this symposium, a professor of Islamic studies held a lecture called "Closer than My Own Jugular," in reference to a passage in the Qur'an in which Allah says that he is closer to each person than their own jugular vein. After the Pentecost service on Sunday, a participant, a medical doctor, told me enthusiastically about this lecture. He said he had thought about the title for a long time and thought about how medically important the jugular is for each of us. It's essential for our survival; our life is tied to it. If it gets injured or bursts, for example as result of an aneurysm, a person can bleed to death very quickly. That's why the jugular may well be one of the most fragile, sensitive parts of the human body. That doctor emphasized how emotionally close the jugular is to him. His life depends on it. The lecture rekindled his awareness of how important his life is to him and how much he wants to enjoy this life, precisely because life can be over so quickly.

This quote from the Qur'an is meant to tell us that God is closer to each of us even than the jugular, this vein of life. Emotionally, that means that humankind feels an intimate connection with God. He is with each person and within each person. In Christian tradition, St. Augustine said that God is "more inward to me than my most inward part."[1] But even these days, church documents often point out that there is a supposed distance between God and humankind, sometimes calling it an unbridgeable abyss. God is the great and magnificent being, while human beings are small and sinful. The image from the Qur'an, though, shows us a different view of God as being more intimate and united with each of us, just as each of us is one with our jugular. For each of us to live, we need the jugular vein, but the reverse is true as well: Without the person, the jugular isn't "alive." Both refer to one another. God without humankind is impossible, as is humankind without God.

In a sermon, one of my confreres once talked about God as "a passionate friend to humanity." He chose this expression based on our use of the word *passionate*. When we talk about a "passionate cook" or a "passionate gardener," we mean a person who invests energy, devotion, and commitment into their job or hobby. God does the same with humankind and his friendship. But in friendship, God cannot be interested in creating a deep gulf between himself and those he befriends.

He can't be interested in distancing himself or keeping himself aloof. That kind of distance comes from the fact that human beings have emphasized humanity's sinfulness on the one hand and God's holiness on the other.

To my eyes, Jesus put special emphasis on God's love and friend-ship for humanity. Despite humanity's weaknesses, Jesus brought every person he met back into this friendship. Whenever he met a person, he called their attention to it and showed them that, whatever they had done or failed to do, nothing stood between them and God. One state-ment of Jesus's that I think gets too little attention is "Very truly, I tell you, the one who believes in me will also do the works that I do and, in fact, will do greater works than these" (John 14:12).

Sometimes I wonder: What would happen in a person if they could allow themselves to think and feel that God has already arrived in them, is with them, is close to them like a best friend, maybe even closer? There are several mystics who have described the relationship between God and humanity in erotic metaphors—full of love, inti-macy, and closeness.

Without being an expert, that's exactly what I think the Qur'an means in drawing a comparison with the jugular vein. God's being closer to each person than their own jugular means he is intimately close to them. This is more a symbolic statement than a biological one. God is close to me because he is also in my body, present and alive in me.

Conversely, that also means that, just like a jugular is essential for human life, God is too. We can call it a jugular, but in Christian terms I might call it the Spirit of God in humankind. God is connected with humankind as closely as we can imagine, and even closer. So, human-kind is not just made in God's image, but much more! Humankind isn't just a reflection of some property God has. God is united with humanity—and I do mean that in an intimate, loving sense. God has the closest possible connection with each of us. He is within each of us.

This is one of the ways in which Christianity really was a revo-lution. In Jesus's day, Jews considered God the Holiest of Holies, far above in heaven. The temple in Jerusalem contained what is known as the Ark of the Covenant, which had inside it the stone tablets of the Ten Commandments received by Moses on Mount Sinai. Those sym-bolized God's presence in the temple, but only the priests had access to the place where the Ark was kept. The idea that God might go "among the people" was practically heresy in the circles in which Jesus moved, and he naturally met with some resistance and opposition. In his very actions and in his understanding of himself, Jesus demonstrates that through him, God can be seen, felt, and encountered as a human being. God wants to be seen, felt, and encountered this way through and in every other person, too. On top of that, Jesus spent most of his time not with the priests and scholars, but with people on the margins of society, those on the lowest rungs of the social ladder.

Paul, one of the most active missionaries for the Christian faith in the first century AD, writes in one of his epistles to a Christian congregation: "Do you not know that you are God's temple and that God's Spirit dwells in you?" (1 Cor 3:16). What had been true of the temple in Jerusalem has now become true of the body of every human being: the body is the space, the site, of God's presence. The body is a divine space. The Gospel of John opens with the well-known sentence, "And the Word became flesh and lived among us" (John 1:14).

This starts out meaning Jesus, but it means Word becoming flesh is supposed to happen in every human being as well. God's Word, God himself, will be seen, felt, and encountered in everyone. The Word with which God created everything in the beginning became flesh in Jesus. That sentence at the beginning of John can also be translated as "And the sound became flesh." Even before God's Word, there was the sound of God, the single note of God in the universe, which then formed and formulated itself into Word. In Jesus and in humankind, God's sound becomes a syllable and a Word. God rings through, not just in the Word, but in the very being of humankind. There's a reason why we talk about speech melody, of the tone in someone's voice, of someone's sound. It's the mood that resonates when that person speaks and reveals whether he or she is speaking from their center; that is, whether that person's speech has "the ring of truth," that he or she isn't just echoing others, but is saying something "all their own."

A human being in their body is a resonator, a "sound-space" in which God can resound and in which that person can discover and find God.

## God Embodied

If the body is a resonator or sound-space for God, or, as Paul puts it, "God's temple," then we should value our living body as the unity of body and soul. In other words, the body I mean isn't just a biological construct whose functions keep the person alive, but an actual being that feels, loves, grieves, and is happy. A person can only express these things via that living body. Today, science understands that anything a person feels or suffers through, whatever brings them joy or pain, is stored not only in the soul but in the body. The living body has organs of memory, too.

But the body was taboo for a long time, especially in Christianity. It wasn't seen as one entity, but as a composite of body and soul. This dualism is based in Greek Platonism and became central to Christian teaching when it was introduced in the Greek cultural sphere. In order to teach the good news of Christian life to the Greeks, the apostles used Platonist terms and ideas, which in turn influenced Christian teaching. That meant that now it was the soul that needed to be saved, to be prepared for and shaped with dignity for everlasting life. All bodily drives and desires, on the other hand, had to be killed off or controlled, particularly the strongest force in a human being: sexuality. Shaping and educating the soul became more important than shaping and educating the body. Taking joy in the body, in food and drink, in emotions and feelings, was considered impious, even though Christianity is really one of the most sensuous of all religions. What else can we see in the celebration of communion, where we share bread and wine, and we taste, smell, and feel God's closeness and love in them?

In body-and-soul dualism, the needs and sensations of the body were ignored, and people were given ascetic exercises. That is largely what leads people even today to think of themselves as creatures with a body and a soul—two separate and competing parts—instead of as one entity.

Today, most people still believe that in death, the body of a person is separated from their soul, which is biologically true. No one is saying that the biological body is resurrected. In the Bible, Paul talks about the body of resurrection or "heavenly" body, which a person is given when the dead are resurrected at the end of all time. In other words, a person will keep living with all their experiences. None of the experiences stored in the body stay unseen, dishonored, disrespected, or unaccepted. For our human lives, it means that body and soul form an inseparable unity: the living body. This body is the home of God.

So, finding and discovering God also means turning toward one's own body, and respecting and honoring it as both a creation of God and a home of God. Accepting it as it is. That also means accepting how it ages, accepting what it becomes over time. Acceptance depends on the life that is expressed; on the dignity that is preserved through all hardship; and on the life experience stored and visible in the body, including in wrinkles gained through worry or suffering.

To me, it's infinitely precious that in a Catholic funeral, the coffin is honored with incense. Incense is made by burning valuable resins. It's a way of saying that this body was valuable. The comforting, cleansing, and healing smell is meant as an expression of the divine healing that is given to all people. This body was a site of divine healing. We need to return to the body, feeling at home in it, and accepting it as our own individual resonating space for God.

In pastoral counseling, people often realize that they have difficulty really feeling themselves in their body, having conscious awareness of it, and feeling at home in it. For me, it's fascinating to explore the reasons for that together and to start to dismantle barriers. It can be interesting to discover one's own body and to pay attention to just how many muscles, sinews, veins, and arteries are in us, and how all of them work together so that we can get up, work, feel joy, and laugh. We can discover how the soul expresses itself in the body. Our body is a miracle with cogs fitting together in fascinating ways. No one in the world exists twice; each is unique in body and soul. Each of us will always be a unique creation of God. That's why what is true of Jesus is just as true of all of us: in him, God became human.

But how can we find a way back into our living body? One idea is meditation. Many people practice meditation these days, and there are many different types and directions. One of the best-known is Zen meditation. Originally from Japan, Zen meditation has also been developed into a Christian form in the West over the last few decades. The basic form of Zen meditation is that the person sits in silence. To do this, I sit down on a meditation stool or pillow. An upright posture with the pelvis as base then allows me to consciously and deeply feel my life surround me. Zen is about being well-grounded in your body, sitting and feeling the resonating space of the living body. Within this space, we feel the presence of God. Often, my thoughts wander or drift away, moving toward the future or the past. As soon as I realize that my thoughts in meditation are no longer in the present, no longer in the simple act of sitting, I try to return to my living body, to be in myself and with myself completely. In meditating, I focus on my breathing and just perceiving my breath. The flow of my breath, and that I feel this flow, brings me back into perceiving my living body.

In Hebrew, breath is called *ruach*, the same word as "spirit." Because *ruach* is feminine, it literally means something like "spiritess." And so in breath, God's Spirit, his or her living power, is flowing through us. Possibly you know that feeling. You're full of strength and energy, creative, centered, at one with yourself, and eager to do things! That is how it feels to be filled with God's Spirit, his power.

Christianity has often demanded the opposite, and often still does demand that we be nice and quiet, fit in, and don't make a fuss. But how powerful must God's Spirit be if it's the force that created the cosmos, heals diseases, drives out demons, and raises the dead! How much power we can feel just by meditating, when we inhale and our chest expands, filling with breath and spirit; when we sit upright and feel God's Spirit flow through our entire body as we exhale! Meditation is a way of feeling ourselves as human beings in the Spirit of God. Feeling our breath is vital to that. We can do that while taking a walk, too, or when we sit in our chair, as a relaxation exercise, or when we "take a breather." Just take a break and take a deep breath.

Here's another idea: Once a week, I meet up with our guests from the *Recollectio*-House at seven in the morning. Unless it's raining hard, we generally go out into nature somewhere. At some quiet, sheltered spot, I then invite everyone to become consciously aware of their bodies. I always start by standing in nature and becoming consciously aware of myself, however I happen to be present this morning: tired, awake, happy, annoyed, or all over the place. No matter how I'm feeling, I have both my feet on the ground. My feet connect me with the earth.

We then go on to imagine that we're firmly rooted to this spot, that we have deep roots in the ground, like a tree. We feel the power of our stance, that we literally have our "feet on the ground," and are literally supported by the earth, by God's Creation. Another part of this is that no one else can stand wherever I happen to be standing at that moment. I'm in my space, and I'm allowed to occupy it. Sometimes I let all our guests spread out their arms slowly, so that they can feel how they reach their full "wingspan." When their arms are stretched out fully, I ask them to feel the power of that stretch, to feel that it is our space, the space we're allowed to take up. It's wonderful when the body can help us realize things that are also metaphorically important in everyone's life, such as feeling grounded and having the room to live and breathe and grow freely.

On top of that, we're also consciously aware of nature. It's wonderful to listen to the birds singing in summer or feel the fresh morning air in winter, and to see the first rays of the sun in spring or hear the leaves falling in autumn. I'm always amazed at how many tiny little noises and sounds I can hear if I just focus on listening. All of that lets me feel myself as a created being, one with nature. By gently touching my limbs—arms, torso, legs—I can feel my living body and the interplay of its parts even more consciously.

Most of the time, we end by touching our head and face with the tips of our fingers as a way of consciously feeling both. As we do, I always make a point of reminding everyone in that moment to perceive their face as an image of God, as the eyes through which God sees the world; as his ears that listen to its worries, joys, and troubles; and as the mouth that tastes and passes on his words. Then we walk silently through nature, feeling the warm sun on our body or meditating on the stream as a metaphor for letting ourselves be carried by the stream of life.

This morning exercise always ends with a bow to God and the Creation and to the group, but also to myself. I bow to the person I have become, to the person I am this morning, through all of my past up to this day, the history of my body, my soul, my life. It's God's history in me, God's history of salvation.

## Self-Acceptance

For a long time, self-acceptance—or self-love, depending on how you look at it—was "underappreciated," particularly in Christian circles. Too often, Christianity was too much about service to your neighbor. Your own needs, of the body and of the soul, weren't allowed to play a role. They had to take a back seat to others' needs. Often, that meant people went beyond their limits of endurance, sacrificing themselves in the end. This happened often in religious orders.

But self-acceptance means accepting yourself in two different ways: accepting your own character and life story, but also accepting your own body. Over the last few decades, I've seen a move to look at the individual, who has needs, capabilities, and resources, and also at the fact that every human being is a work of art and beautiful for that reason. Of course, I may think someone else is ugly, but this opinion is based more on my own ideas of what is or isn't attractive. As God's unique creation, however, every human being is beautiful: each of us has the face of God, and out of the eyes of each of us, a bit of his love shines. It's just a question of looking.

It's very important to me that in my monastery we emphasize the individual development of each monk. Everyone gets the help he needs to fulfill himself. Over twenty years ago, when I was still a student, I visited the monastery for the first time and was charmed to meet so many young monks who appeared so alive, completely comfortable with themselves. But to feel comfortable with myself, I first need to accept myself, with all the good and the less good. When Jesus says, "You shall love your neighbor as yourself" (Matt 22:39), that's exactly what he means. I can accept myself just the way I am—inside and out. I'm allowed to accept the way I look, even if I maybe wish my nose looked a little different or my stomach had some more muscle. And I'm allowed to accept who I am, who I've become through my very own story. Both aspects, external and internal, are hard for many people, especially when a life story contains hard or painful experiences. It often takes years of intensive counsel and companionship for a person to accept themselves.

Self-acceptance isn't something that happens when someone tells you that you need it. Every person needs to build up their own relationship with themselves, with their life, story, and body, in their own time. During that process, they're allowed to recognize that trying to change everything all at once is overwhelming. Some changes can only be made step-by-step. Every person needs to follow their own rhythm, the speed of their own soul. Particularly in this context, the biblical stories in the beginning of this book are practically archetypal. Every biblical figure had their own "cross to bear." All of them had to learn how to live with their own hardship, to integrate it into their life while still knowing themselves to be accepted and loved by God. Abraham suffered from his childlessness, Moses from the fact that he had killed a man, Joseph from his suspicions of Mary's infidelity, Mary from the burden God had placed on her, and Zacchaeus from not being seen and liked. There's a German phrase that translates loosely to "An 'Oof' under each roof." It means that every house, every family, every home has some hardship to deal with, even today, be it a blow of fate, an illness, a brewing conflict, unemployment, financial problems, or worries about children, grandchildren, or aging parents.

These problems often carry a social stigma, too, and the people affected would rather keep up appearances than admit that they've lost a job, or been divorced and left with the children, or suffer from a potentially fatal disease. But that means that they're not just left alone with their worries, but also use up incredible amounts of energy and strength trying to playact for the people around them, trying to pretend that everything is A-OK. The thought isn't just "What will others think of me?" but "What will I think of me? How can I live with myself, now that I'm unemployed, sick, or alone?"

It's an important step for a person to accept themselves fully, without needing to hide or sugarcoat anything, whether from themselves or from others. I find it helpful to remember that God is inside every human being and that humankind is made in God's image. God continues to turn toward humanity.

Whenever we have a hard time accepting our own fate in life, especially when it comes to social stigma, it can help to look at the Bible again. God's arrival in Jesus happens in a stable. Joseph, who has probably received judgmental looks because of Mary's pregnancy with a baby that isn't his, now must stand by while the baby is born in some "horrible hole" of a place. Might he have felt humiliated, brought low? Would it have been easy for him to accept this situation? And how Mary must have felt! But the Three Wise Men who arrive "ennoble" this birth and show Mary and Joseph and us that this stable is a place of royal dignity. However dirty it may be, no place is unworthy of God's presence. And through that presence, the people who live even in the lowest places are worthy of royal dignity.

I recently read a text by the German mystic John Tauler, about "manure":

> Take an example from horses in the stable. Their manure is filthy, and it is offensive to the smell. But the same horse that makes it, draws it with great labor into the fields and there it makes fine wheat and rich wine—all the better wheat and wine for the filthiness of the manure. Thus mayst thou use those disgusting faults of thine which thou canst not quite overcome. Scatter them upon the field of God's holy will and abandon thyself very humbly to His loving care.[2]

If the manure from the stable is brought out to the fields or into the garden, that's often where the most beautiful flowers grow. It's a good fertilizer. This shouldn't be taken for too easy a reassurance, because it's a very deep idea: God knows no place, no person who is unworthy. No one should be ashamed of their story, their path, their body, or feel so much fear that they lose their hope in the future. It can be so good when a person is just allowed to tell their life story without being judged, without immediately being bludgeoned by moral outrage. There's no place in the Bible where we see Jesus dig around in someone's past or ask someone what they did and didn't do. He just encounters people in the moment and takes them as they are. Several times in the Bible he asks, "What do you want me to do for you?" In other words, "What is supposed to happen here; where should perspectives open up? What do you need to get healthy, or what do you need to accept yourself the way your life is now and the person you are now?

The other thing this shows is that one can't approach everyone the same way. That's why Jesus asks, "What do you want me to do for you?" He doesn't show up with the answer ready, doesn't show others what they're supposed to do. These days, we get plenty of those suggestions on the one hand: "Eat healthy, get enough exercise, and don't drink too much." This always makes me feel that everyone except me knows what's good for me. On the other hand, Jesus looks people in the eye and asks them what they want, hope, or believe they need for themselves.

In our monastery, we sometimes describe it like this: ninety monks, all of them in the same black robe, but with ninety different heads sticking out of it. This is where Christianity has a deep message, for every single one of us, with all sorts of different needs and wishes, is respected in their uniqueness, as a unique creature of God and a unique dwelling place for God. In his *Rule*, Benedict tells the abbot of the monastery that what does one person good can be bad for someone else. It's the abbot's job to recognize what each person needs for their soul and living body to be saved and to develop their full potential, to everyone's benefit. For Benedict, the abbot is like a doctor and the monastery like a space in which everyone can develop, in which everyone is accepted with their weaknesses, in which everyone is seen as "holy dwelling of God," in which everyone strengthens everyone else.

In that sense, a monastery is a protected space that can't be translated exactly into the "normal" world, and yet every monk is invited and has a duty to pay attention to himself—his own body, potential, and gifts. The goal is knowing who I really am, what my limits are, where I am overwhelmed, or rather let myself be overwhelmed, and where I need to rethink, and then to find out what it is I need and want right now. But it's also an invitation to take joy in life, in indulging, in oneself.

A lot of people come to us to experience just that: finding themselves, their living body, their soul. They want to accept their own history and discover all the things that are possible, to wake up all their sleeping potential.

## Human Beings as Cocreators

Today, we have a special responsibility for the Creation. God saw everything that he had made, the Bible says, and indeed, it was very good. The Creation is not here by accident. Life is meant to develop on Earth; humankind is meant to preserve the Creation, to multiply and to take joy in God's Creation and in each other. Everything that lives on earth pulsates with God's life force and Spirit. His breath of life doesn't breathe only in the living body of human beings, but in everything that lives. Again and again, all creation wants to live and grow. No one has described and expressed this urge to live more strikingly and credibly than St. Francis of Assisi. He saw all creation as praise to God: the birds with their songs, water with its life-giving force, fire with its warmth, the rich soil, the sun with its light, and the moon and the stars with their clarity at night. All these things praise and exult God. Francis calls them all "sister" or "brother." He feels a deep connection with each, since they are all creatures of God, just like human beings.

In today's world, in which everything is possible and human beings don't have to rely on the rhythm of nature for survival, because we can either grow or import whatever we want, we also need to relearn our respect for and connection with nature. We're responsible for the fact that all creation supports life, gives nourishment, and enables procreation.

In his much-noted encyclical *Laudato si'*, Pope Francis emphasizes this responsibility of all humanity. Creation is not the result of random chance, because it was made by God and therefore has divine dignity that we are to preserve, no matter what. As the place of God's presence, as the place where God's Spirit lives and breathes, a human being is part of God's creative Spirit. The Spirit that lives in me and you is the same one that called everything into life and, in the beginning, floated above the chaos and ordered everything. In a way, we can say that each human being is a kind of cocreator, someone tasked by God with shaping the divine force within him or her, giving God a form in this creation. Through these cocreators, God wants to become tangible and felt as someone who wants life. This creative force that humanity carries within it can be a way for each human being to find God within themselves.

When Jesus breathed God's Spirit into his disciples, he wanted to fill them with God's Spirit of life, with which he was filled himself, so that they could go out into the world and let God's divine power take shape in the world, to continue his mission and keep building what he called "the kingdom of God." Shaping the world is therefore in the hands of each human being, and that includes shaping the world and society to be more just. No one lives only for themselves; no one on earth is alone. Each one of us has a responsibility to ensure that the Creation and life on Earth can keep living. Each one of us has a responsibility for making sure that people can live together in peace and justice, especially given that each of us is in the image of God. Every single one of us has responsibility for others just as much as for ourselves.

An old Christian prayer says,

Christ has no hands but our hands
to do his work today.
He has no feet but our feet
to lead men on their way.
Christ has no lips but our lips
to spread his story wide.
He has no help but our help
to lead men to his side.

That's what matters: using our own hands—our feet, our lips, whatever potential we have—to build a more just world in God's creative power. The German poet Angelus Silesius writes,

And were Christ born in Bethlehem today,
but not in you, you would be lost always. (*Cherubinic Wanderer*, I 61)

It is about this birth in us, about the question that St. Francis of Assisi asked: "What do you, God, want me to do?" How can Christ become human today through me? How can he grow visible, be born into this world? What matters is cultivating an attitude of creation, is feeling and recognizing the divine strength that lives in each human being and how it can take concrete shape in the world.

# FINDING GOD IN OTHERS

So far, I've focused on finding God in ourselves. But if God is present in every human being, we can find, discover, and see him in others, too. This is the theme of the next sections.

## Encountering Others

From the very beginning, the God of the Bible shows himself as a god of dialogue, someone who looks for contact with a person and engages with them in dialogue. Sometimes he talks to them directly, and sometimes he sends an angel as his messenger, to bring news or a message to someone. But the really new and revolutionary thing about the New Testament is that God himself comes in the shape of a human being. He comes to earth as Jesus to be as close to humankind as possible. When he does this, it's not about bringing new commandments or a new message. He just shows humanity very specifically what he meant in his words, what it means to live according to his commandments.

So, if I'm trying to find God in others, my best "treasure map" leading me to God is what Jesus himself said and did. As a human being, he lived among us like any other person. He loved, suffered, and argued as we all do, but he did some things differently than what people back then were used to. He also looked at things from a completely different point of view, which didn't just surprise the people who encountered him, but sometimes also irritated or frustrated them. But that's part of encountering God as well. Sometimes it's uncomfortable in one way or another. It's never about setting the status quo in stone, but about changing the world and making it better.

In what follows, we'll look most of all at how Jesus acted in our world and what that might mean for us today if we want to try to find

God in others. But first, let's discuss one of the Old Testament's most impressive passages, where God engages in dialogue with a human being and lets himself be moved: Abraham's negotiation with God over Sodom and Gomorrah. Today, we still sometimes say that it "looks like Sodom and Gomorrah" somewhere, as the name has become synonymous with degraded morals, disorder, and chaos. In his dialogue with God, Abraham asks whether God would destroy the city even if there are as few as fifty righteous people in it. God answers that in that case, he would let the city stand. But Abraham keeps negotiating, until in the end, even ten righteous people would keep God from destroying the city. Here, God lets his heart be moved and shows himself to be "big-hearted." Abraham dares to have the dialogue, to negotiate. That should encourage us to know that human beings are allowed to argue with God, are allowed to speak with him, to communicate. All 150 psalms of the Old Testament are prayers in which God is accused, praised, and thanked, all in the knowledge that all of us depend on him. In the end, God has control over life or death, but he does allow us to speak with him, to find him in dialogue. And he, for his part, answers.

Jesus later takes this up and shows that, in his deepest nature, he is someone who always engages in dialogue with others, who talks with them, even argues with them, answers questions, and speaks words of encouragement and healing. Whenever he enjoyed a meal with his friends or let himself be invited into a village, he entered into a relationship with people by way of dialogue and communication. That signaled to the people around him: "You are important to me." That signal is the beginning of healing. A person can only heal and get healthy if they trust the doctors and people who are treating them. Jesus always healed people in dialogue. Sometimes he started by asking what he should do for them and only then healed their illness with decisive words. He also entered into a dialogue with the unhealthy forces inside a person, called "demons" in the Bible's worldview.

But often, he healed through nonverbal communication, that is, through touch and skin contact. Today, we know how important touch can be for healing, when nearness, connection, love, and care aren't just expressed in a verbal dialogue, but through the body. The body can't lie. Body language is more real and truthful than quite a few words of some verbal communication.

This nonverbal communication includes so-called signs or symbols as well, such as we find, for example, in the Eucharist, a meal in which bread and wine are shared with a nonverbal meaning. When people congregate in Jesus's name and share a meal just as he did so many times, that's a sensuous experience, transmitted through taste, touch, and smell. There's communication among the people participating, too, just by sharing food and drink. Christians break bread and drink from the same cup. That's a way of expressing what our deepest faith is. Sharing the things that people need to live is the foundation and center of their faith. That doesn't mean just food, but also a word of comfort or encouragement, or a touch or hug. All those are things we need to live, and God is present within all of those. He is right among us.

None of the stories in Scripture makes this as clear as the encounter on the road to Emmaus (Luke 24:13–35). After Jesus's violent death, two of his disciples are traveling to Emmaus. They are grieving, depressed, and devastated. They had put all their hopes in Jesus. He spoke of God so lovingly and intimately, so differently from the scribes and priests. While they are traveling, Jesus joins them, but they don't recognize him. He explains to them why he had to die, why all the things they have experienced in Jerusalem had to happen. When they reach the next town, the disciples ask him to stay with them. When he sits down with them to have dinner, takes the bread, prays, and breaks the bread, as he has done with them so often, they recognize him and now know that he is alive.

This gesture of breaking the bread is so typical, so unmistakable — it can only be Jesus. It's in this experience of his presence with two people when an encounter with the divine follows. This encounter can happen wherever people share life with one another. The stories of Easter may talk about it, but the central experience is that right there among human beings is a force, a love, a power that we can call divine. This power lets the fearful set out, heals the sick, and lets people spend their lives spreading his message, even today. We can find and experience God in others in both verbal and nonverbal dialogue, a dialogue that warms, strengthens, heals, lifts up, and does not judge or discriminate.

Christian theology teaches about the Trinity, God's threefold nature based on three divine persons: Father, Son, and Holy Spirit. Its details are complicated to explain, but what it really means is that God is in relationship. Each human being is invited into this unity of successful divine communication. It is said of Jesus that he spoke as if by divine power. People who feel connected to God and the Divine Spirit can be like that. Those who listen to them feel that "here God is coming toward me."

## Loving Others

One of Jesus's most significant statements in the New Testament is his answer to the question of which commandment is the most important. The Gospel according to Matthew says,

> When the Pharisees heard that he had silenced the Sadducees, they gathered together, and one of them, a lawyer, asked him a question to test him. "Teacher, which commandment in the law is the greatest?" He said to him, "'You shall love the Lord your God with all your heart, and with all your soul, and with all your mind.' This is the greatest and first commandment. And a second is like it: 'You shall love your neighbor as yourself.' On these two commandments hang all the law and the prophets." (Matt 22:34–40)

Here, Jesus mentions the love of God and the love of the neighbor in a single breath. The two commandments are linked in themselves. God has made humanity and humanity is his image and dwelling place. Whoever honors God and recognizes him as the Creator of human life must also acknowledge and respect his creatures in the same way and recognize God within them. That is why Jesus sets both commandments on the same level.

But then this commandment of love applies not only to God and to me, and not only to that one beloved person whom I have as my partner in life, but to all people everywhere. Personally, I find it tricky to "command" someone to love, at least emotionally. It's clear that we can't like every single person, much less feel an emotional attachment to them. But what we can do is to acknowledge the other as a being of God, one who has just as much of a right to live on this planet as we do, and whose life should be protected unconditionally, just as written in the constitution of my native Germany.

In his story of the Good Samaritan (Luke 10:25–37), Jesus expresses this clearly. The story is very well known, so the provocation it contains is often ignored, maybe also because Jesus's listeners would have understood the background and societal context much more clearly than we do today. In the story, a man on a business trip is mugged, beaten, and left lying in the road. One after another, three people pass by. The first two—a priest and a Levite—don't have, or more accurately, don't take the time to help him. The third—a Samaritan—helps the man, brings him to an inn, gives the innkeeper money for his care, and tells the innkeeper that when he (the Samaritan) returns, he will pay back the innkeeper any additional money the innkeeper winds up having to spend on the injured man.

The provocation in this story happens at two points. First, both the priest and the Levite had to know what they should do. As scholars of Jewish law, they knew the commandments of brotherly love. They might have thought, we could speculate, that the man lying in the road wasn't their brother at all because he didn't belong to the same tribe, which is how "brother" was understood at the time. It applied to all those who were "like me." But the Samaritan, in the eyes of the Jews listening to Jesus's story, would have been an unbeliever, a heathen, yet he does what the commandment asks: he helps, without thinking about the injured man's social standing, religion, or nationality.

In this story, Jesus is clearly criticizing the Jewish scholars, and additionally setting up the unbeliever in contrast as a true believer, who has really understood and applied the commandment that the scholars constantly preach.

The second provocation comes at the end of the story, when Jesus says to the man who asked him about the most important law, "Which of these three, do you think, was a neighbor to the man who fell into the hands of the robbers?" The teacher of law answers, "The one who showed him mercy" (Luke 10:36, 37).

The emphasis stops being "Who is my neighbor?" There are ways to wriggle out of that question, and see only your family members as neighbors, for example. The question instead becomes "How can I be a neighbor to someone else?" When I recognize that someone else needs help and I am willing to help them, that person becomes my neighbor, or rather, I recognize the neighbor in that person, and I must help that neighbor unconditionally. This shows something psychologically, too, because the other person is always also a mirror for me. In other words, my behavior toward someone else always says something about my behavior toward myself. If someone denies help to another person, what does that mean for the help that person needs? For myself, do I accept the help that I need? Do I pay attention to whether I'm getting the help I need?

What matters is a fundamental attitude of solidarity toward myself and others. That's exactly what Jesus means when he says, "And a second is like it [meaning just as important as the commandment to love God]: 'You shall love your neighbor as yourself'" (Matt 22:39). I can have solidarity with myself. That's a learning process, too. If I have solidarity with myself, I can have solidarity with others as well. If I know where I need help, I can approach someone else in their need for help. None of us can achieve or manage everything all on our own. No one has every talent and ability, and, if we hit our limits, we need others' help.

The early church had a sentence that I think is valuable: "A single Christian is no Christian." That's not to devalue the individual, but it does make clear that it takes two or more to be Christian. Jesus says, "For where two or three are gathered in my name, I am there among them" (Matt 18:20). When he sends his disciples out into the world, he sends them in pairs. People can give each other strength and courage and lift each other up and complement each other. Yet there are also people who find it hard to admit their own weaknesses and accept help. They immediately feel worthless, like they have failed or like they're making the same mistake over and over again. So sometimes a person can only feel their own limitations, their own needs, and their own need for help; when their body goes on strike, it "pulls the emergency brake" by breaking down or collapsing. That's when we realize that, however hard we try, we can't keep going like this. In the church, it used to be completely normal to place heavy burdens on people, to demand that they keep improving themselves morally forever, and that they live pure and irreproachably. In a way, what was preached was that human beings had to work hard climbing up the ladder by accomplishing extreme feats of asceticism. But it's much truer that God comes toward us along this path, that he accepts us just the way we are, in all our weaknesses and need for help, in our limitations and imperfections.

Jesus's words make this clear when he talks about the burdens that priests place on the people but can't fulfill themselves. He says it even more clearly when he says that they preach water to others, but drink wine themselves. Or he says that the priests untie their mules and oxen on the Sabbath, so they can drink, but forbid healing on the Sabbath (Luke 13:15). He doesn't, however, let that stop him from healing on the Sabbath, and doing so often. The priests see this as dishonoring the Sabbath by not resting. Jesus doesn't mince words when answering, "The sabbath was made for humankind, and not humankind for the sabbath" (Mark 2:27).

To Jesus, healing people is a service to God. It's a way of honoring the Sabbath, since God doesn't want people to bring him sacrifices or follow rules for the sake of rules. He wants them to be healed, to have health in body and soul. Even in the Old Testament, there are fantastic, deeply moving images showing God's devotion, his unconditional engagement with humanity, and his wish to lift up human beings. These "ways of behaving"—the ways God interacts with human beings—show us today how we can interact with one another in "godly" ways. It shows how we can let the love that God has for all his creatures shine out in our interactions with others. Isaiah 42:3 says of the messenger God will send into the world that "a bruised reed he will not break."

This makes it clear that God wants to approach humanity in order to heal and lift up people. A person who hits bottom, whose fate has hit them hard, someone close to desperation and unhappy with themselves, that's the kind of person God wants to lift up, to encourage with new hope. That should be the fundamental Christian attitude as well, that a Christian helps lift up the person on the ground, raising up someone who's down, strengthening and encouraging the hopeless.

In another example, the prophet Elijah flees, because God has proved his strength against Baal, and now Elijah is being chased. When he has no strength left, Elijah sinks down under a broom tree, gets lost in depression, and just wants to die. He falls asleep, and when he wakes up, there is water and a fresh-baked loaf of bread next to him. An angel commands, "Get up and eat, otherwise the journey will be too much for you" (1 Kgs 19:7). God, in the form of the angel, doesn't criticize Elijah or lecture him for not continuing. He sees that Elijah needs strength, and so gives him food and drink. Anyone who has ever been on a long hike, or who has gone walking in the mountains, knows how refreshing a sip of clear water from a brook or spring can be. That is not to mention how comforting the smell of freshly baked bread is. It literally gives us strength to keep going, strength to live. God helps us and looks at what we need to keep walking our path.

In the story of Jonah, God gives his prophet the mission to announce to the city of Nineveh that unless it repents, it will face

God's judgment. When Jonah finally accepts the mission, the city does repent, but Jonah is annoyed and feels insulted that God spared the people in the city and was lenient with them. In the end, he sits down, as Elijah did, under a bush, tired and depressed. God let the bush grow so that it would give Jonah shade from the sun. The next day, when the bush withers, Jonah complains loudly to God, but God says he doesn't understand. Why is Jonah angry about the demise of the bush, but he wouldn't be angry about the destruction of the Ninevites and all their livestock? Not only is God kind to people, he also cares about the animals, as they also have dignity and rights as creatures, and people have duties to animals. Judgment is never God's goal, nor is it his inner wish to punish human beings. He is kind! His categories for acting and thinking, and for dealing with people, are different from those of Jonah. Lifting people up and encouraging them is much more important to God.

That's also how people are allowed and supposed to encounter each other. The other person is supposed to be uplifted, encouraged, and strengthened. In his *Rule*, St. Benedict writes that the cellarer of the monastery, if he needs to deny a fellow brother a request, for example, if that brother wants to buy or requisition something for himself, should first explain his denial and then give him at least a good word. That isn't meant to be a cheap consolation. How important a good word can be! Whether it's a simple "Good morning," an unexpected call, or a short greeting from a person we hold dear, we all know how much good a little word like that can do us.

The same is true of real, deep comfort, which doesn't need to be a big gesture or a lot of words. Sometimes what a person really needs is just for somebody to be present so that they can feel that "I'm not alone." When I'm accompanying someone spiritually, I sometimes mention that idea and ask whether they have a best friend they can call day and night. It is so valuable to know that I have somebody who will go through thick and thin with me. No matter what happens, when I call and need that person, they're there for me. As an emergency counselor, I see that again and again. People are always thankful for my just being there. In the first minutes and hours after an unexpected event, most often the sudden death of a person through an accident, heart attack, or suicide, friends and family members often feel lost. They're grateful that there's someone there who can be by their side and give them a sense that they're not on their own. For me as a counselor, that's always also the confirmation that God won't leave you alone. He is carrying this suffering with you. He can bear it, and that help is for all people. I never ask about their faith, religious denomination, or even nationality. We also have contacts with other spiritual counselors from other faiths with whom we can get in touch.

Here, too, it doesn't matter whether I personally like a person who is in need. That person is in the image of God and has dignity that can't be taken away. In that person, God is asking me for my help, and, in the help that I give, the person can feel God's care. In this world, God doesn't have any arms or hands for helping, except those of his human children.

# Community as Church

It would make sense if the church, as the herald of God, standing in his service, were the main place people experience God, encounter him, or recognize God in encounters with one another. But these days, I often get the feeling that in the Catholic Church (the only one for which I can speak), the focus is on self-administration to maintain the status quo. Its figureheads tend to live in a kind of clerical narcissism. This is true even though the church is meant to be an *ecclesia semper reformanda*, a church that always must reform, or renew, itself. It should be constantly going back to its beginnings, literally, to its original form. It is called to think back to what it actually is and how people should experience it as a space where God is present. In Ancient Greek, the word for "church," *ekklesia*, originally meant just the group of people who assemble around and in God. Out of the idea of the people of God in the Old Testament, a group who belong to him and that he journeys with, a new people of God gradually grew. Jesus wanted to renew the people of God, a group he was part of as a Jew, but not to found a new church. From the beginning, the shared meal was the central celebration of the early followers of Jesus, who came to be called Christians. Christians met at first in small groups in their homes, and with their families, and did just what Jesus did: they shared a meal, breaking bread and drinking wine together.

For Jesus, it was practically a "trademark" that he shared bread and wine with the kind of people we met in the story of the encounter on the road to Emmaus. He did that with those people who were outcasts, whom the law teachers thought weren't worthy, those God

46

supposedly rejected. That was the provocative thing about Jesus, that he dared to speak about God, dared to stand up in his name and claim his authority. All of that was taboo for Jews. That God might become a human being, might show himself in a person, encounter humanity as a human being, engaging with humankind and showing unconditional solidarity with the rejected—all that was unimaginable at the time.

Add to that the encounter in a meal, when Jesus gives himself as food to others, and says, "This is my body, which is given for you. Do this in remembrance of me" (Luke 22:19). In Aramaic, Jesus's native language, the word for "body" means the whole person, that is, the body with all its feeling, thinking, and acting. So, in giving the people with whom he is sharing a meal his body, he is also giving them his love, kindness, nearness, and solidarity. He does this to make clear that in the same way people need bread as food, they also need this meal, as this divine message is nourishment for their soul and sustenance for the path ahead. The meal is an expression of intimate connection with Jesus, with God, even if after his death and assumption, he isn't visibly living among us with his body anymore. This is the meaning of the experience at Emmaus, which is so hard to put into exact words, but some other force journeys with humankind. When people remember Jesus, by talking about what he did and said, then he is present. That was and is sustenance. That also leads to a solidarity in everyday life, in following Jesus and living together in the community as one feels during the meal. The people with Jesus, who ate from the same bread, felt connected like a single body: "Now the whole group of those who believed were of one heart and soul" (Acts 4:32). The early Christians didn't feel this connection only with each other, but with everyone else as well.

Jesus extended the commandment of love by giving his followers the task of loving their enemies. He gave them the realization that whatever they do to someone else, including and especially someone who is suffering, they are doing to him as well. This makes it clear: "I encounter you in the other people around you." What radical solidarity! And how different an image of God that reveals than the one Jews had at the time, with God sitting high in heaven, unreachable by humanity, with even his name not allowed to be spoken. Jesus, on the other hand, said that God shines in everyone. In each person, we can see the face of God. The person next to us is our brother, our sister in humanity. That is the good news!

This God doesn't let himself be boxed in or pinned down. He doesn't stop at the borders of churches. There is a round that sings, "Every part of this earth is holy to God's people." God breathes in every place, in every person, in every bush. God's Spirit blows where he wills. I am convinced that a church that calls itself the church and the people of God needs to be inviting, needs to be conscious of the fact that God is present in everyone. Or to put it another way: *church* doesn't just explicitly mean the community of people who believe in God and Jesus as his son. Instead, church is where people come together, where they encounter one another as people seeking God, as people who long for God, who ask questions, and who can't define God exactly, but who believe in the thing all religions share: love.

Church is wherever people are on the trail of God and his love. And however much opinions differ on individual points, what is important is God's fundamental message: he is here, he supports us, he walks with us, and he strengthens and encourages us. Whoever wants to find him must find humanity.

# To Find God, Seek Humanity

I remember once accompanying a group of students and parents on a pilgrimage along the Camino de Santiago, also known as the Way of St. James. In a monastery where we stayed overnight, I was asked whether I could hold the evening Mass, which included a sermon. Because I didn't have much time to prepare, what I said was off-the-cuff. While I was talking, the following sentence formed inside me: "God in me encounters God in others." The Bible has a deep story that puts just that into words, when Mary, pregnant with Jesus, goes to visit her cousin Elizabeth, who is pregnant with John the Baptist, Jesus's forerunner. John the Baptist will later proclaim Jesus as the Redeemer and Messiah.

Because Elizabeth is almost ready to give birth, while Mary is still in the early part of her pregnancy, Mary wants to help her cousin Elizabeth and be by her side. Elizabeth says, "As soon as I heard the sound of your greeting, the child in my womb leaped for joy" (Luke 1:44). What an expression of joy as if John had heard, even in Elizabeth's body, who was coming to visit him and his mother. If I look at both children as divine children, God in Mary is encountering God in Elizabeth. In a manner of speaking, everyone is pregnant with God. God is in them because they are in God's image, and because they have the divine mission to discover God within them and bring him out into the world, to make God visible in this world for all humankind.

In our *Recollectio*-House, where we offer, among other things, long-term courses for people who work in the church but who are in crisis or need some time away from work, each guest has both a thera-peutic and a spiritual companion. At the beginning of these courses, people often ask, and with good reason, what the difference is between spiritual and therapeutic companionship. In my conversations with the people at the course, I first work with whatever the guest brings with them. That can lead a conversation in a more therapeutic direction. In the same way, a therapeutic conversation can include elements of spirituality. All the guests have a background in spirituality and Chris-tianity, and work in and for the church, so God and the church play a big role in their lives. But a conversation only gets explicitly "spiritual" when I start bringing in the perspective of God. I ask where, in the ongoing process, God is showing himself, or where the guest perceives and feels him, where and how they can find their way to God, and where they are finding God in themselves. Where is God giving them the strength even for difficult steps, and where do they get the energy to make the tough choices they have to make? Or where are they real-izing that God is always with them, walking beside them, never taking back his affirmation of their life. But my job as a spiritual companion is also to become the midwife for the person by helping them reach a new dimension of their journey or their being, to bring God back into awareness in a different way, to help them discover him newly and dif-ferently, just as a midwife brings a "child" into the word with care and attention to the person giving birth.

I remember Christian youth retreats I went on as a teenager. Every evening, there would be a discussion on some topic about faith. We had a lot of time to ourselves, but also went on some outings together. Slowly, I began to understand that these retreats were structured in such a way that at the end, you were meant to turn to Jesus Christ. There was always an evening in which Jesus's death and his suffering for humankind was illustrated in its excruciating length and drama. The goal was that every person present would feel their sinfulness, see the need for their personal redemption, and be convinced then and there to repent and accept Jesus Christ as their Savior. The whole thing always included a specific mention that otherwise one would be lost and destined for hell. A lot of pressure had built up.

It's God's nature to walk with people, to be within them and always reveal himself in such a way that they can recognize and understand him and his mission. His goal is not to make them fear hell, but to let them discover that he loves them, goes with them, and can be a supporting reason for their life. He follows each person, finding and addressing them. In doing that, he can be pretty stubborn, making himself heard again and again, until the person discovers his presence and answers it. This is what happens to young Samuel in a story in the Old Testament. Samuel's mother, Hannah, has consecrated him to God out of gratitude and brought him into the temple to serve there. At night, on his bed, he hears a voice calling him. He goes to the priest Eli, his overseer, but Eli says he hasn't called him. This happens three times before Eli realizes that God is the one calling Samuel, and that Samuel should answer, "Speak, LORD, for your servant is listening." Samuel does as he is told, and God calls him to become a prophet. God persistently calls attention to himself, following Samuel until (with Eli's help) Samuel understands who is calling and for what purpose (1 Sam 3:1–21).

The way I see it, the way of teaching faith I experienced when I was young has nothing to do with being a midwife or finding God in others. It is more about deception. The organizers wanted to make me compliant and receptive with day trips and free time, and maybe they even wanted me to feel bad for being ungrateful if I had enjoyed the outings but rejected the "indoctrination." Rather than being a midwife, this kind of faith-teaching felt to me more like trying to pass off a stranger's child—an idea of piety that wasn't my own—as mine and trying to make me care for it.

Being midwife to someone else also means accepting their path, their way of walking, and their speed. Even if I can see God in another person, it still makes a difference whether that person can see that God is in them, doesn't know it yet, or is only just starting to discover it. It's about bringing *their* "child" into the world, whatever wants to become and grow clear in them, not what I am imagining or want to communicate.

Whether I'm encountering an atheist, a deeply faithful person, a seeker, a questioner, or a doubter, all of them are a space for God's presence; all are images of God. Or to put it another way, the other person is a burning bush. In the burning bush, God tells Moses his name: Yahweh, or "I am who I am." This "I am" is a promise God makes to everyone: I am here. Especially where another person is really burning for something, where they are enthusiastic about it, and where they put all their passion into something, that's where we see God and his passion for life revealed. That's where what has always been inside someone is expressed. It's easy to see this kind of view as "taking over" the other person.

Who am I to say someone has a "quality" that they may not want to have and that they're never consulted about, but it is just assumed as the way they are? This is a question of faith, and of every individual's own view of the world and of faith. In conversations preparing for baptism, I often encounter the view that through baptism, a person becomes a child of God, that God will accept this tiny human being as his child. The baptism consciously invites the child into the congregation of the faithful, but that child has been a child of God since birth. Actually, it's been a child of God ever since God began to think this person, thought of him or her. This view would be possessive and restrictive if it defined a person instead of leaving them free, if it made the person a prisoner of a system of morals, dogma, and rules, where that person was forced to believe in God and follow the rules of the faith.

But God is a God of freedom. To this day, the sacraments of the Catholic Church, such as a marriage, don't count if they are forced. The person receiving them must decide of their own free will. As ever, in the Catholic Church, conscience is the highest good and final authority.

Now, if I see another person as a space in which God is present, and if I recognize their face as a unique face of God, I am according them dignity and a call to freedom. That person is meant to shape their life in freedom, to say yes or no, and to use or waste their talents and abilities. As a companion, I can then offer them this idea as a path, and that person can then choose to discover it for themselves. This takes a weight off their shoulders, because they feel that they're allowed to take their own path, at their own speed, and with their own thoughts and feelings. It can be freeing because the goal of this undertaking is open. I'm not telling them what the result is supposed to be or dictating that they have to find God.

Sometimes I think how liberating it could be if the church finally started helping people to be strong and independent. This would mean that the church would see every one of us as an individual creature and image of God, walking our path in the strength of God. Instead, I get the feeling that the church is still trying not to give anyone too much space, too much self-assurance, or too much strength. They might get the idea that they're important—too important, more important than others! Especially within the hierarchical thinking of the church, we shouldn't underestimate the role that kind of thinking plays.

In religious orders, I see the same thing at work in a different way, especially during singing or prayer. Here are twenty or thirty people all in one place, who have decided to dedicate their entire life to God and his good news, and when they praise him, they sound like a choir of church mice! And I think, "Where is your praise? Where is your strength for thanking God? If God is the foundation of your life, where is your rock-solid praise, your full-throated thanks, and the joy that rises to the heavens?"

One of my confreres once talked about God's "I am" in his introduction to the daily service. He parsed it as "I am here," and mentioned that we confirm this exactly three times in the Mass: in the introductory rites, before the Gospel reading, and during the blessing. At each point, the priest tells the congregants, "The Lord be with you." It should be "The Lord is with you." I see that as another sign of church hesitancy, worrying that there just might, somehow, somewhere, be some lone person with whom God isn't. The people reply, "And with your spirit." Which means, "Yes, that's how it is, and the Lord be (is) with you, as well." Only after he had explained this, did my fellow brother open the service with that sentence. The convent answered a little hesitantly, and my confrere said, "That was a bit weak—one more time!" So he repeated the greeting. This time, the response was stronger. God is strong and alive and wants to express himself in ways that are strong and alive, so that others can realize and sense that God is present here.

Sometimes I meet people who are afraid that if they find their own divine power, discover and allow God's fire and passion inside themselves, if they enter into their strength and uprightness, others will see them as egotistical, individualistic, or self-aggrandizing. They've internalized this idea that above all, a Christian should serve and not care too much about him- or herself. But as human beings, we're allowed to look at ourselves and see that God is there, that God is burning passion within us, and that he is exactly that in others, too. In *A Return to Love*, Marianne Williamson says,

> Our deepest fear is not that we are inadequate. Our deepest fear is that we are powerful beyond measure. It is our light, not our darkness that most frightens us. We ask ourselves, "Who am I to be brilliant, gorgeous, talented, fabulous?" Actually, who are you not to be? You are a child of God. Your playing small does not serve the world. There is nothing enlightened about shrinking so that other people won't feel insecure around you. We are all meant to shine, as children do. We were born to make manifest the glory of God that is within us. It's not just in some of us; it's in everyone. And as we let our own light shine, we unconsciously give other people permission to do the same. As we are liberated from our own fear, our presence automatically liberates others.[3]

She encourages us to trust in our own greatness because God is shining in us. Jesus emphatically says, "You are the light of the world" (Matt 5:14). That's not a call but an affirmation! He doesn't say, "Become the light, try hard to be the light despite your weakness." Each human being is a space for the presence of God. We are the world's light! The real question is whether we human beings can accept this greatness, and how we see ourselves. Seeing ourselves as small is not in God's interest. God himself thinks great thoughts of us and wants to do great things with us. This view can liberate us as well. If we're aware of this gift, we can also allow greatness in others. We can grant them their greatness without needing to make ourselves small. God's greatness in a human being never comes at the cost of others. No one is greater or lesser in his eyes. No one has a higher or lower standing. In and through each person, God wants to shine out in this world.

Again and again, I talk with people who compare themselves with others and feel small because everyone else seems to have more talents, be more popular, and more visible or well known. We don't need to compare ourselves with others but can take joy in each other and in the fact that God has made it possible for us to let the light shine through us into this world. We can allow ourselves this and choose that greatness. If we do that, others in our presence will find the courage to make this choice.

## As You Did to the Least of These, You Did to Me

When Pope Francis was elected in 2013, he began his first address from the balcony of St. Peter's Basilica by telling the crowd how the cardinals had called him from the other side of the world. We don't know whether, in that moment, he felt like he came from the ends of the world, but soon after his election, he made "outsiders" one of the main themes of his papacy. He spoke of the church as a field hospital, which has the task of treating wounds and healing people. He said that, metaphorically, the shepherd in the herd of God should smell like the sheep, and that he preferred a "bruised" church to a congregation of saints. In all these images, he has expressed that the church is real for him when it approaches people who live on the margins, who have no real place in today's culture of achievement and perfection, who have no voice and are therefore easy to overlook or push out. What an uproar there was, almost a scandal, when Pope Francis visited a prison on Holy Thursday of 2014 and held the traditional foot-washing ceremony, washing the feet of male and female inmates, even those who weren't Christian but Muslim!

Washing the feet has been a deep sign for a long time, more so during Jesus's time than today. Back then, people went barefoot most of the time, or maybe wore sandals, and therefore tended to have dirty feet from all the sand and dust of the street. On the one hand, washing removes that dirt, but it also means touching a person at their lowest point, where one tends not to look, not even at oneself. During the washing of the feet, though, all the dirt and dust is washed away. Jesus always, figuratively speaking, washed other people's feet, because he accepted every person in their deepest nature, with all their "dirtiness" or "uncleanness," offering them cleansing, care, and love.

What a sign that the pope restarted this tradition in his own way! Until recently, that service was generally held in St. Peter's, with the pope washing the feet of the priests. But now, Francis goes to a prison, instead of to the basilica, and washes the feet of prisoners instead of priests. With that gesture, he made his understanding of discipleship to

Jesus clear, by going to the "real" people on the margins and, no matter what they have or haven't done, giving them back their dignity. In the pope's view, a church that follows Jesus Christ belongs with the people who live as outsiders, not in the dome of St. Peter's.

If we look in the New Testament, that makes the pope a radical follower of Jesus, because Jesus was the first to go beyond the "borders" and "red lines," to enter "no-go areas." He wanted to show people that, no matter where their life led them and what margins they wound up in, God is by their side in solidarity. People who used to be shunned by society for being supposedly "rejected by God," and who had therefore become sick in the eyes of their fellow human beings, are the people Jesus befriends and whom God puts first. Jesus's speech known as the "judgment of the nations" also makes this clear. When most people hear the word *judgment*, they often think of some harsh decree handed down by a person over someone else. But what the word actually means is a "justification," a way to make just, to lift up the lowly. Humanity is put back in its proper place and the world is put back in order.

When Jesus announces that, in judgment, the good will be separated out from the evil, what he means is that God's view, the good, just view, will be stronger. Everyone who was treated unfairly will receive justice, and everyone who behaved unjustly will be put in the right place and will recognize their injustice. In that speech, Jesus lists people who today are outsiders living on the margins:

> I was hungry and you gave me food, I was thirsty and you gave me something to drink, I was a stranger and you welcomed me, I was naked and you gave me clothing, I was sick and you took care of me, I was in prison and you visited me. (Matt 25:35–36)

Over time, these words of Jesus became what is known as the works of mercy, *mercy* being the word that describes the essence of Jesus's actions and therefore God's. The Hebrew word for "mercy" is *rachamim*, related to the word for "womb," indicating that mercy describes the qualities a mother shows to a child in her body: warmth, nurture, protection, and care. Mercy means the unconditional care and love God shows each person. I have come to appreciate the fact that in the counseling we offer at our abbey, whether in the guesthouse, individual conversations, courses, youth work, or the *Recollectio*-House, the person visiting us is never judged. Anyone who comes to us as a guest receives the same unconditional care and attention. Their life story is what it is. They came in with it and receive warm, human care. The goal of our counseling is to learn how a person who has come to us can find their way back into a life that fills and fulfills them, that satisfies them, that lets them (re-)discover the deepest foundation of their life, where and however it is revealed to them.

In an earlier section, we looked at that experience in stories recorded in the Bible of people who were found by God. God shows himself and finds the person, no matter whether that person is a murderer or a saint. He shows himself particularly in people who need help. In them he waits for merciful love—in the hungry, the thirsty, the stranger, the naked, the sick, and the imprisoned. At the end of his speech, Jesus says, "Truly I tell you, just as you did it to one of the least of these who are members of my family, you did it to me" (Matt 25:40).

I'd like to look at each of these groups of people and the works of mercy more closely, connecting each of them with our own lives, because merciful attention to others always begins with myself. A person who can't be merciful toward themselves, who can't care for themselves in a loving way, will find it hard to do that for others.

## *"I was hungry and you gave me food"*

One out of nine people all over the world does not have enough to eat, and more people in the United States live in poverty than in any other wealthy nation. What frightened me was when I thought about how quickly a person with a secure life can wind up on the streets through divorce or job loss, needing to beg for their daily bread. Hunger is one of humanity's greatest problems. The world has enough resources to feed everyone, but the problem is in the distribution of wealth. While supermarkets in America are overflowing, people in Tanzania get one warm meal a day if they're lucky, and that meal always consists of the same ingredients: maize porridge with some vegetables. What an injustice!

Jesus's call to feed the hungry in service of God doesn't mean that any individual human being is meant to solve the problem of world hunger. Each of us is only expected to do whatever is in our power. For the problem of hunger, that means I can ask myself how much I eat, what I eat, and whether I am eating healthily and giving my body what it needs, no more and no less. But also, I can consider what food companies and politics I am supporting with my purchases, and what I can give others, whether as a financial donation or in form of food that I am giving the needy or a food bank. I recently read online that a woman had canceled her wedding, and because it was too late to cancel the catering, she and her ex-groom invited homeless people to eat food at the expensive wedding reception.

Of course, hunger can also happen on the level of the soul. What are we hungry for today? What does our soul need? Looking at the number of people who visit our abbey as guests, there must be many people who are feeling hunger in the soul, for a spiritual dialogue in which they can speak freely and find their bearings again. Even if church seems to be playing a smaller and smaller role in society, that doesn't mean that people today have fewer spiritual needs. Exactly the opposite! It may just mean that many people don't trust the "official" church with the answers to the questions they have, because they see it as out of touch. I think many people trust monasteries in a different way because they see them as an "other-space." Maybe they get the impression that people in religious orders live their principles more authentically. Or they trust monasteries because they can come and go just as they are, without anyone making a moral claim on them.

In my own life, I can ask, Where am I an outcast? Where am I leaving myself behind in the margins? And in this case, where do I get my sustenance? What nourishment does my soul need? How can I turn toward myself and nourish myself? How much love and care am I giving myself?

In our *Recollectio*-House, we see it as our mission to help guests focus on healthy self-care. That means recognizing my own needs and looking at possible ways of taking responsibility for them. We can't always delegate that responsibility to others. This is a real challenge, especially for people who have chosen to live life without marriage in the church. What keeps our own soul alive and our body healthy? How can I rediscover the joy in life and make myself alive again? We shouldn't be too quick to answer these questions spiritually or "piously." If God made humankind, he wants each human being to be alive, to take joy in life. In that case, anything that gives a person joy in their life is a deeply spiritual and pious act. What nourishes my own soul? That's a question that everyone needs to answer for themselves.

## *"I was thirsty and you gave me something to drink"*

Scientists predict that the next major wars and conflicts will be over access to water. When water resources grow scarce, and droughts get longer and longer, everyone will fight to have enough to drink. This thirst may cause another series of refugee crises, with people fleeing to water-rich regions and countries. I get the impression that the world is trying to marginalize this problem, too. Whenever I read that the United States is building a 13-billion-dollar warship and Germany intends to increase its military spending in coming years, I wonder whether at least a part of this spending should be invested in the solution to these problems. We live in a country where we (mostly) still have enough water and expect it to flow freely when we turn on the tap, which means each of us has a personal responsibility for how we use water as a finite resource.

But once again, the questions here are also, What is each person thirsting for? Do I know and understand the worries, sufferings, and thirst of my neighbor? What does each person thirst for in their soul? How can I help them? What are the clear wellsprings from which they draw their life, which, after watering the soil of their soul, will bring forth blossoming? How can they feel God flow through their life again? The same is true of my own life. I can ask all the same questions of myself.

I remember a song that was popular when I was doing youth work in the church and that today is still sometimes sung on our retreats. The chorus is "I am still thirsty, I still have dreams, I don't want to be satisfied so easily." I think it's a great gift whenever a person can be satisfied with their life. But it's just as important to keep one's thirst for life, for aliveness and personal growth. It sometimes frightens me when I meet older people and get the feeling that what's most important to them has to do with having their everyday life up and running and having everything going just as they're used to. In our monastery, we Benedictines also live a life that's highly shaped by the recurring daily rhythm of prayers and chores. The point of this routine is the stability and dependability it gives us. But that inner longing, the inner thirst for life and for God are crucial too. I need to keep asking myself, What are my dreams? What is God dreaming in me?

## *"I was a stranger and you welcomed me"*

Being a stranger is the fundamental experience of the people of Israel. For several hundred years, they lived in Egypt as strangers. Then God shows himself as a liberator for the first time, bringing them home, even though they must travel through the desert for forty years. Today's Christian conception of God as constantly walking with each person, by their side, is founded in this time of journeying through the desert. The people of Israel know what it means to be strangers somewhere. Anyone who has traveled during a vacation, or even who has gone to a different town, knows how good it can be, as a stranger, to be welcomed with joy and an open heart, to find a home somewhere. On vacation, we generally prebook everything, including our "home away from home." But pilgrims, for example, don't book anything beforehand. Wherever they've arrived that night is where they look for a place to stay. When they are welcomed, they feel joy.

The same is true on an even deeper level for the homeless. How good it must feel for their body, their soul, to find a shelter, or for a doctor to offer their services for free when they—the strangers right in front of our eyes—need attention and care. I ask myself, too, how can I help them? There is a story by Rainer Maria Rilke. During his student days, he walks through Paris with a friend, the same streets each day. One day, Rilke gives a rose to a homeless person he sees begging at the same place every day. After that, he doesn't see the homeless person for a week. One day, he is back at the same place, and Rilke is asked by his friend what the homeless person lived on for all that time. Rilke answers, "On the rose." Which means that the homeless person lived on the care and attention connected with the gesture of the rose; the feeling of being seen, not only in his physical needs but also in his emotional needs. Here, a person who was also emotionally homeless received emotional care.

Sometimes when I see a homeless person, I'll buy some food and bring it to them. That often leads to a good conversation. It may only be a drop in the bucket, but for at least a few moments, a person who is brought low and has no place they can call home has received physical and emotional nourishment. Everyone needs this kind of attention and the physical and emotional home it provides. But here too, I can only do what is possible for me in my surroundings. I'll never be able to give a home and food to all the homeless in this world. Jesus always encountered individual people and then asked them what he could do for them. He paid attention to each individual person he met and helped them specifically. He never spoke in general terms or gave general instructions that "people should start doing" one thing or another. This attitude that Jesus held can relax us. I can't rush to help every person in the world, and I don't need to. I can help that one person I meet on the street, on the path I am traveling, at work, or wherever it may be.

For me, the questions can be, Where am I homeless? What parts of me need a home, need attention and care? Which parts of my personality am I shutting off, am I trying to ignore? Where and how can I feel home, and experience emotional warmth? How do I receive love? Can I turn toward myself and do myself good?

What probably moved the world most throughout the autumn of 2015 was the refugee crisis. On no other subject was German society, in which I live, as divided. Chancellor Angela Merkel's sentence, "We'll manage it!" remains on our minds even today. At the time, there was a lot of discussion about the term "culture of welcome." While one-half of our citizens demonstrated loudly against the refugees and called for a quota on refugees let into the country, the other half got to work. An unprecedented wave of solidarity could be seen and felt. All around our monastery, many were willing to give material donations; but there were also many volunteers for teaching language classes, helping refugees deal with making trips to state offices or looking for housing, long-term jobs, or training. Today, the topic is no longer part of the everyday news cycle, but that doesn't mean there are no more refugees. Ever since the closing of the Balkan route and Germany's agreement with Turkey, the numbers of incoming refugees have gone down, but many people are still coming.

We naturally ask how much help and solidarity are possible. I believe that we can do more than many people think. We saw it in 2015. I was moved by how nonbureaucratic and quick the abbey's decision to help was, and how natural it was for us to take in people without even looking at their nationality, religion, or culture. When Mary was pregnant with Jesus, she and Joseph had a completely different experience. They set out from Nazareth, where they lived, to Bethlehem, because there was a census during which every person had to be counted in their place of birth. But Joseph and Mary could not find a place to stay, and so in the end they had to bed down in a stable, where Mary gave birth to her son. They experienced firsthand how it feels to be traveling and denied a place to rest, to be unwelcomed. Mary and Joseph show us, in the eyes of every person who is fleeing and looking for a safe place to stay or at least rest, God's eyes looking to us for help and a welcome home. They look to us to give warmth for body as well as soul.

To my confreres in the abbey who care for the refugees daily, it's deeply fulfilling to feel the thanks they give in a look, a word, a gesture. I'll never forget the images of the refugees we took in when they first arrived at the abbey. Many had nothing with them but a plastic bag carrying what little they owned. Some had only the clothes they were walking around in. Nothing else. How much it meant to them that after weeks and months of fleeing, after imprisonment, uncertainty, and fear for their lives, they could finally find a safe place, a bed, fresh clothing, and food.

But why do we react so fearfully and defensively to the topic of migrants and asylum seekers? Why do so many have this fear of "foreignization," the fear that the West could become Islamic very soon, or that the United States won't be a white-majority nation anymore? I think that there are many different reasons at work. As recently as my own youth, life (at least in rural areas) was still shaped mostly by the church. Everyone went to services, became an altar boy (if Catholic), and celebrated the holy days with feasts, processions, and pilgrimages, where everyone sang with the full conviction of their hearts. That was our faith, and within that faith, we kept to ourselves.

When I went to study at university, I encountered a very critical position on the church. There were calls for reforms within the church and the development of what we today call individualism. Globalization opened up society, loosened up rigid structures, and showed us a larger point of view. Traveling and seeing other cultures became more widely accessible to people. That made our own convictions more unstable as well, because they weren't the only ones we had ever encountered. We got to know people who believed in something else, in a different God, and were still kind people worthy of love, who treated others with respect. That's something that not everyone had been able to imagine before. At its root, anything foreign we encounter makes us question whatever is familiar. Unlike on vacation, where we can take other, stranger cultures as broadening our horizon, when we see it lived out in our own country, we experience the stranger's culture as a threat. On vacation, we get a snapshot of what that culture is and can go back to our own culture. But at home, we can't sidestep other cultures anymore. We meet them on the street, when we go shopping, around town or at least in the city. We are forced to engage with the culture, to form an opinion, take a position. People who come from a different culture, belong to a different faith, or have different traditions make us question whether our own faith is still fitting, whether it's "right." Many of us just got handed down our faith by parents, for no other reason than that our parents lived it and always preached it as the only true and right faith.

Not least, contact with strangers therefore confronts each human being with all the things that are strange to us, where we are strange to ourselves. Sometimes people say that they don't recognize themselves in how they behaved in some situation or other. Or others say, "That's not how I know you! What's going on?" What aspects of our own nature are foreign, strange to us? What parts of ourselves do we find unpleasant?

I'd like to circle back to my time in Tanzania. Being there was the first time I felt how different—how foreign—my own socialization was. Tanzania had hardly any paved roads. People walked barefoot, and I hardly ever saw anyone in sandals. Many people lived in mud huts or shacks made from corrugated iron or similar materials. Women carried heavy loads and had a completely different standing than they do in our Western societies. And I kept being confronted with the really primal forces, like the blooming of nature seconds after rainfall and wild animals that I had only known from zoos walking around in nature. I witnessed archaic rites, such as a group of young men who drummed themselves into a trance for hours before a soccer match, or women who sat before a house where someone had died, making a funeral feast and wailing and singing songs of grief for hours. All these experiences seemed to move me into contact with all the archaic, primal, "wild"-seeming forces and rites that slumbered in me too, underneath my "Western facade."

On top of all that, the people who come to us today from the Arabic or South American spheres tend to have grown up in a patriarchal culture, meaning a male-dominated society and (at least from our Western point of view) the subjugation of women. In our society, we mostly reject that, and we have the feeling that we've "come farther" than they have. We're more developed, have higher standards, are wiser, and maybe even feel like we are better people. But we haven't nearly achieved equality either! How can men today integrate their own masculinity, their masculine strengths? Where and how do women live their femininity today?

I meet a lot of men who may be good and successful at their jobs but have an incredibly tough time taking a clear position in their relationships, truly relating with their partner, engaging with them, or entering into a dialogue with the woman or man they love. This is another situation where experiencing a different social organization can often make us question our own social order, our own growth, twice over. First, are all the things we think of and preach as "right" actually as right and absolute as we always claim? That is, are we truly convinced, and do we stand behind them? Second, is what we call true on paper also consistently turned into everyday reality so that equality in our own country has come as far as we like to think?

In African and Arabic countries, homosexuality remains taboo as well, often forbidden by law. That raises other questions for us: How do we ourselves deal with the idea? Are we actually as tolerant as we like to pretend outwardly?

The question is what parts of us do we find foreign or strange. What sides do we deny, even though we suspect that they exist? Where am I sometimes a stranger to myself? What parts of myself am I afraid of, or afraid of admitting? What image of myself do I have, and where do I not live up to this image? Where do I feel I need to be a certain way because others expect it, but actually I'm different, and want to be? Where am I pushing myself into social roles or predetermined expectations? Where do I feel alienated because I'm not in touch with myself?

In other words, where am I fleeing from myself? Is there something like an inner homelessness, like being a migrant from my own self? Where have I become alienated, a stranger to myself, because I am miles away from anything that I dreamed for myself and my life?

In those cases, finding a new home, feeling welcomed, means finding the way back, going on a journey (back) to myself, making a new home for myself in me and in my own living body; making a new home for myself in God because he welcomes and accepts me.

## "I was naked and you gave me clothing"

When we accepted the first refugees in 2015, there was a big wave of solidarity. People from surrounding towns donated many things they no longer needed but that were extremely valuable to the refugees: clothing, bicycles, furniture. Today, there are many places where needy persons can get clothing and other items of daily life.

For us as individuals, this can be the call to go through our own closet, see what we no longer wear, and decide what we could donate. Everyone can ask themselves, What can I do without? What is unnecessary? But there's another challenge in how clothes are manufactured today. We can ask in what condition people in other countries most often work to produce clothes for us today. It's almost impossible to research all the various working conditions. In the same way, it's almost impossible to buy only clothes that were produced in fair and just conditions. In addition, today many people have to buy cheap clothing, because they don't have a lot of money to spend on it.

That's another part of being a human being in today's world. We're linked into chains of production and trade with conditions that are virtually impossible for us to influence, even though they're unjust and exploitative. We need the products that big corporations make, and we have to recognize that we're a part of unjust systems. But we can still try to use our influence to change the things we do have influence over.

I see the mission Jesus gave us to clothe the naked as a mission for the soul as well. How many people are emotionally "stripped," that is, have their protection taken away and their privacy publicly violated? We all probably know the feeling of being embarrassed by others, whether through a prank in school or pictures that were never meant for the public but were posted anyway. Newspapers compete for the best scoops on the private lives of celebrities. This is shameless exposure of people's private lives and a violation of their personal privacy.

But there are also people who volunteer to be in shows based on "emotional nudity." Examples of that are shows like *Big Brother* or *American Idol*, where young people agree to have their every action judged by self-proclaimed professionals who seem to want to crush contestants' self-worth with a single sentence. Why do people volunteer to go through something like that? It may be a need to be a part of something, to participate, to have one's own life story in the limelight for even a few minutes, to be heard. Is it a need to have someone, anyone, pay attention to how one's life currently is? Perhaps we can also understand it as a "naked" person's cry for help for someone to come and clothe their soul, for someone to come and care for them and protect them. With many of these people, you get the feeling that they don't have any real friends and no one who wishes them well, but that they're surrounded by people to whom they are somehow useful. In that case, clothing the naked would mean being an honest friend to such people. And that can sometimes mean talking about what does them good and what doesn't.

Even in talk shows, I often have the feeling that the goal is not to look at objective information on certain topics from different points of view and hear well-reasoned opinions. Instead, it's about who can yell loudest or talk over others most. Everyone's right on principle, and no one seems able to distance themselves from their opinion. Every opinion has to be defended to the death. That kind of environment says a lot about the respect and mutual regard going on in the studio. Devaluing others, not letting them finish their thoughts, ridiculing them, and insulting them are all forms of trying to show them up, "expose them," in other words to metaphorically, emotionally strip them naked.

Especially in situations like that, people whose soul has been hurt need words, sentences, and gestures in which they can clothe themselves, the kind that warm, heal, stabilize, and protect their soul. As previously mentioned, St. Benedict in his *Rule* compares the abbot as leader of the monastery with a good doctor who knows how to treat wounds. The abbot's job is to make sure his monks can become whole and healthy, that the wounds in their souls heal, and they can gather new strength and hope. That has to be the most important thing. On his office door, my supervisor once had a poster advertising a therapists' convention. Today, it hangs in my office because to me it expresses wonderfully how I see my role as counselor. The poster says,

Send smiles
Awaken hope
Take away fear
Conquer doubt
Experience joy
Offer trust
Give love
Feel confidence
Use strength
Share happiness

If by counseling and companionship I can give people the gift of a smile, awaken hope and trust in their own path and in God, that act is like a warm coat I can spread over their wounds, injuries, and nakedness. For me, an impressive example is Jesus's healing a man in the temple on the Sabbath. That man's hand is "withered," probably meaning paralyzed. Jesus says to him, "Come forward!" (Mark 3:3) and heals him. By doing so, he is taking the man out of the margins where his illness, which was considered a punishment from God, has placed him. Jesus gives the man attention and care that clothe him in emotional warmth. He knows how long this man has been socially isolated and how long he has seen himself as rejected by God. Jesus wraps him in the cloak of mercy, closeness, and healing. How happy that experience can be, when people blossom and come away from an encounter with a little more hope, a little more confidence, a little more trust and comfort. Hopefully, they go away a little more healed.

For me, the question is, Do I know anyone who has been emotionally exposed in this way? Who in my own environment may need this kind of attention, may need healing encounters and experiences? How do I actually talk with other people? Where do I use words that hit home, hurt, expose, and let others "stand naked"?

According to Benedict's *Rule*, in a monastery, the idiosyncrasies of every person should be respected, and this idea is part of that, recognizing and feeling how I communicate with others, how I practice criticism, and how I tell them something that may be difficult to hear so that they can accept and take in what I am saying.

In my role as guide and emergency counselor, I hear a lot of stories about how insensitively some doctors or police officers brought people difficult or life-changing news. These doctors and police officers, instead of communicating empathy or even compassion, gave them the impression of just wanting to say what had to be said and then leaving as quickly as possible. The people who received the news were left feeling alone and unprotected—"naked."

For me, part of that also includes how we talk about other people. I'm thinking about the famous "talking about others behind their back," when we say bad things about someone, and they don't even get a chance to hear or defend themselves. It's just as much an act of disrespect, devaluation, maybe even emotional exposure, whenever we spread or pass on information that someone told us in confidence. Instead, it should always be about preserving the other's dignity and developing a feeling for where they hurt, because in that, too, people can be very different in what they feel.

Another question is, Where and how do I clothe and protect myself to keep potential injury away from my soul? How do I care for myself if I've been emotionally hurt? When I feel that I've been hit hard by words or something that's happened, it's important for me to offer myself attention and respect. Sometimes the words that have hurt me keep nagging at me and develop a life of their own. Then I wind up thinking, "It's true, I really am worthless, and this other person is right, I've just made this or that mistake yet again." In that case, it can help to be aware that I shouldn't let it get to me quite so much. I don't let those words or thoughts penetrate my soul. I imagine an inner stop sign that clearly forbids these thoughts and words from entering any closer into my soul.

If I can manage to do that, then possibly I can also make clear to the person who said the relevant words how much they hurt me. It may then turn out that that wasn't their intention at all, and that person only now realizes how hurtful their words or actions were.

## "I was sick and you took care of me"

Taking care of the sick has been a Christian task—a task specific to Christianity—from the very beginning, always linked with the conviction that in the sick person, God or Christ himself is suffering. The creed states that God is omnipotent. God is all-powerful, strong, capable of influencing, guiding, and controlling the fates of the world.

In the Old Testament, God is often on the side of those who win. Victory over enemies is always a sign that God is with the people who win. I believe that what's being expressed here isn't so much God himself as someone's idea of God. Before Jesus, it was unimaginable for God himself to also be weak, vulnerable, sick, suffering, much less that in the shape of his son he would wind up on a cross and die. God knows what weakness is. He himself felt helplessness in Jesus's vulnerability. That is why he is especially close to people who suffer.

I encounter God in these people, but also whenever I allow my own weakness and vulnerability. This acceptance may even be a prerequisite for accepting weakness and vulnerability in others and seeing God in these qualities. I often meet people who have difficulty acknowledging to themselves that they are vulnerable, that they have been hurt. Allowing and perceiving these injuries is the beginning of healing and transformation, of allowing oneself to be the person one really is. Paul writes, "Whenever I am weak, then I am strong" (2 Cor 12:10), because it's exactly in that moment that God's power can work to raise me up and make me conscious and strong. That may sound like a paradox, but it isn't. God is weak *and* strong. He is both the one who suffers and dies in Jesus as well as the one who has the strength to save him from death and give him new life.

So where do I find the "sick" aspects of my own life, even if I am physically healthy? Wherever I look for my own vulnerabilities. Care always also means a dialogue with the person I am caring for, making contact with them. If I take care of my own vulnerability and get in touch with it, I may be able to find out what has hurt me, what keeps hurting me, what wounds want to heal without being torn back open, and what wounds want to be perceived and communicated. The goal of this is to treat my own wounds. The fatherly and motherly sides are allowed to comfort the weak person that I also am. I can let myself be embraced and feel God's care for me, knowing that, just like a mother or a father, God cares for humankind. I don't need to hide my wounds from him.

## *"I was in prison and you visited me"*

As of December 2016, a total of 2,162,400 people were incarcerated in the United States, while 6,613,500 were under the supervision of the U.S. adult correctional system.[4] I remember when I was studying in Münster, I was living in the seminary, together with a priest who worked as spiritual counselor in prisons. He told me a lot of stories about the people behind bars and what experiences he had with them, including their resocialization. An impressive part of the German criminal justice system is reintegrating people into society, making it clear to them that in secular law, their actions have consequences and are punished. After this punishment is completed, however, they have the possibility of returning to society. How different this is in countries with the death penalty. Apart from the fact that, in my opinion, no human being has the right to deny someone else their life, the death penalty also makes it impossible to take back a judgment, or to rehabilitate someone. The death penalty seems like a way to get rid of crime once and for all, to banish it from the community with force, and, where necessary, with violence. But that is never how it turns out. Instead, the real question is what crime says about society itself. What causes it?

Having completed my studies, I worked in a home for difficult children. This home had a separate section for those who were choosing this home instead of a jail sentence. It really was a "closed unit," the children and teens were locked in their rooms at night. They were permitted to leave only under the supervision of nursing staff. On the one hand, I was shocked at the criminal histories these young people had. One was twelve or thirteen and already the head of a car smuggling ring. On the other hand, I was also shocked by how incredibly socially isolated some of them were. There were adolescents whose parents wanted nothing to do with them, not even visiting on Christmas or sending a letter or package. I'll never forget how one of these young people sat in front of the television one Christmas Day, watching a cheesy movie. In that moment, I didn't see a criminal, but a person, who was still almost a kid, desperately screaming for and deeply in need of love and care. It was clear to me how much these people, who maybe had become criminals because of a difficult family background, longed for love, protection, family, and acceptance, just as you and I do. The criminal is one side to them, but just one. Each of these children and adolescents is also a human being and deserves a chance. That's why it's so important to me that forgiveness is such a central theme of Christian faith. When Peter asked Jesus how often one should forgive, he said, "Not seven times, but…seventy-seven times" (Matt 18:22), meaning infinitely often. Yet we so often ask ourselves, "How many more chances should I give this person, how often should I forgive them, how often can I let myself be taken advantage of without breaking from it?"

Whenever the media report on cases of rape or abuse, which is always also a massive emotional injury and nakedness that victims often carry with them for the rest of their lives, there are always voices crying for revenge against the perpetrators. Sometimes they call for the death penalty (or its reintroduction, in countries where it's been abolished). It's part of the Christian faith that even a person who has committed an atrocious crime should get another chance. That is their challenge, too, a sizable part of which is that the person who acted criminally has to find peace with themselves, forgive themselves, and decide to find a new path, to step out of the spiral of crime. Forgiving oneself doesn't mean sweeping everything under the rug and just forgetting, but actually facing up to the responsibility, recognizing one's own actions and their causes, accepting legal repercussions, and looking to the future.

A few years ago, I read a book of reports by counselors about their experiences on the front lines of spiritual guidance. A prison counselor wrote about a prisoner, describing vividly how in prison this young man decided to study theology and become a priest, and the great joy he felt when the bishop gave his assent. The counselor took in this man when he had weekends on parole, giving him his trust. He was not disappointed. Whenever this young man visited the service, the counselor got the feeling that during communion, Christ—and thus God himself—was laying himself in the man's hands. Don Bosco once said that "each saint has a past, and each sinner a future." No one has no faults; no one is just holy. In my actions toward others, I'm also always showing my actions toward myself. There's a good reason why Jesus emphasizes that love for our neighbors is connected to love for ourselves: "You shall love your neighbor as yourself" (Mark 12:31). If I can't accept myself, then I can't accept anyone else, either. This means that part of our mission when we visit and care for the imprisoned is to accept our own flawed nature. Benedict instructs the monks, "The way to become holy is…by never despairing of the mercy of God"[5] (*St. Benedict's Rule*, 4:74).

God's mercy is always greater than all mistakes, all weakness, all self-recrimination, and all inferiority complexes. Just like our own vulnerability, we can also sit with our own flawed nature to embrace and accept it. That action contains the impulse for a fresh start in repentance, which succeeds when we presume that we are fine, as we are. We need to practice this view again and again, toward others and toward ourselves.

Visiting the imprisoned can also mean solidarity with all those who feel an inner imprisonment, who feel paralyzed and can't find a way out of the habits and patterns that are making them suffer. In conversation, I often see people who don't have the strength to step outside of their problems and take steps toward a solution. They feel a need to talk about it but continue to feel imprisoned in the pattern. My job is to listen, to care about them, and offer them attention. Or it is to absolve or bless them. Sometimes it takes a great deal of patience before an inner crack opens up and a person dares to step out of their inner prison.

For my own life, the goal is to visit with my inner imprisonment and look at it, closely and honestly. Where am I imprisoned in myself?

Where do I want to be freed? In what external circumstances do I feel trapped? Often, the way out is hard. The Acts of the Apostles says that Peter, sitting in prison because he proclaimed how Jesus returned from the dead, is visited by an angel and freed from prison. Unfortunately, that's not how it is for most people. The reason is often that they actually feel pretty comfortable in their "life prison." It may limit them a bit, but it's also familiar, while anything new is unknown and frightening. That's why Jesus asks the sick, "What do you want me to do for you?" What he means is, Do you actually want to become free? How the Israelites grumbled on their way out of Egypt, saying, "If only we had died by the hand of the LORD in the land of Egypt, when we sat by the fleshpots and ate our fill of bread" (Exod 16:3). They may not have been doing well, but at least they had enough to eat. Setting out requires leaving behind one's own comfortable existence.

## "You gave me a dignified burial"

The Christian tradition has added burying the dead to the "works of mercy" in Matthew 25. This is based on the conviction that in death, a human being retains their dignity, as a human being and as a space for God's presence, a divine temple. As such, every human being deserves to be buried with dignity.

In the Christian faith, death is the transition from earthly to eternal life. When I have offered spiritual companionship to the dying, I have found that it strengthened my faith, because precisely in dying, we encounter God. It is moving to see how people, when their death is not sudden, relax more and more as they let go, and sometimes even have a smile on their lips in the moment of death. I remember a confrere who, when he was sick, and I asked him whether he was ready to go to God when he called, answered, "If I hadn't been ready for that, I shouldn't have entered the monastery." After his death, the confrere who had been at his side recounted that he had died during the *Suscipe*. The *Suscipe* is sung during profession, when a monk gives his vow to stay in a monastery his whole life, and he says, "Receive me, O Lord, and I shall live, and let me not be confounded in my hope."

This is sung with outstretched arms, expressing that the monk is putting all his hope in God. As he was dying, my confrere, who was already unresponsive, held his arms in that position, ready to be

71

accepted by God. In my fellow brother, I could feel that God was coming toward him and sending an angel to ease the transition.

By honoring funeral rites, we have a chance to express that the departed person was of the earth—completely human—and is now given back to the earth, but that God dignified them by making them a space for divine presence. God communicated himself to the world through them. On the eve of the funeral, it's a lovely tradition to come together and tell stories out of the life of the departed, with everyone recalling what they know. In this storytelling, God's work in and through the person shines out. Each funeral, each memorial, speaks of faith's hope that God will grant humankind everlasting life, however that may look.

Sometimes I am astounded to hear that in hospitals or old folks' homes, funeral home personnel are allowed to come only at times when residents won't see or encounter them. This shows that people can't or don't want to engage with the thought of death. Death is blocked out and pushed to the margins. Instead, we keep looking for ways to get younger, to hide the signs of age, and to find the gene for long, if not eternal, life on earth. But engaging with mortality, making ourselves aware that we will die, is our chance to confront ourselves with the questions, "What do I believe?" and "What is my hope?" Grappling with these questions can mean touching on or finding the divine, and so finding a dimension of being that goes beyond our own mortality.

St. Francis called death "Brother Death," and Benedict, the saint after whom my monastic order is named, is patron saint of the dying. All this accepts and welcomes death as a natural part of life. Death is given its due as a part of my life that ends my biological life and leads me into a new way of being.

A person's death is the ultimate borderline moment. The dying person goes to the borders of their earthly life, which is a fitting way of putting it. Whenever we cross a border on earth, we enter a new country, where we meet other people living in a different culture from ours. Our perspective, our horizon of experience, widens. In the same way, a dying person is entering a new land, going from earthly life into a new, heavenly life. The process isn't really death—an end—but a transition into a new, different form of existence. In Christianity, people believe that this border crossing more than any other leads people to encounter and experience God. We talk about seeing God face-to-face.

In the burial service, we sing the words, *"In paradísum dedúcant te Angeli...et perdúcant te in civitátem sanctam Jerúsalem."* Translated to English, it means, "May angels guide you to Paradise....and lead you into the Holy City of Jerusalem." In the Judeo-Christian tradition, Jerusalem signifies the home of God. The process of dying has several stages, and it takes time for a person to accept the inevitable and come to terms with it. This is part of the reason we sometimes talk about a "death struggle."

There are also other situations in the life of a person that offer borderline moments and that can be an extreme challenge for that person. They can lead to an experience of God as well. I'm thinking of my novitiate, for example, during which I had no contact with the outside world. Or other situations where life confronts people with tasks that seem far beyond their own strength. Then sometimes we get the feeling that we can't do it, that we won't make it, and we ask ourselves, "Why did I choose this situation for myself?" But suddenly a new dimension with new horizons opens up inside us, and we realize we can do more than we thought. We feel a strength or force come toward us that can help us master the situation. Of course, there are also always situations in which we need to respect our limits, where it's clear that if we keep going now, we'll lose ourselves or our health. That's another kind of borderline situation that can help us experience God, because we need to grapple with our own weakness, with not being able to do what we wish we could. It's an existential confrontation, and we ask, "What supports me? What defines me? What am I worth? Who am I? What if I can't do what I most want to do in the world?"

Many people keep trying to work against that confrontation, sometimes by looking for eternal life that steals people's mortality, or by other ways of pushing our own boundaries and trying to be productive, young, and dynamic even longer. Grappling with my own boundaries can open the gates, open my eyes to the approach of God, whether in death or in other "low points" of my life, where I let myself be held by God and can accept my own limitations. That's why borderline situations tend to be ones of dying, of letting go. Applying the idea of "burying the dead," I may need to ask myself, "What part of me wants to die, wants to be let go? What borders in my life should I respect, and what borders should I transcend?"

# Notes

1. St. Augustine, Bishop of Hippo, *The Confessions of Saint Augustine*, trans. Edward B. Pusey, DD (Grand Rapids, MI: Christian Classics Ethereal Library, 2005), III.vi.11, www.ccel.org/ccel/augustine/confess.iv.vi.html.

2. John Tauler, "The Yoke of Christ Is the Soul's Thought of God," in *Sermon for the Fifth Sunday after Epiphany*, trans. Walter Elliot (Washington, DC: Apostolic Mission House, 1910), https://archive.org/details/TheSermonsAndConferencesOf/page/n179.

3. Marianne Williamson, *A Return to Love: Reflections on the Principles of a Course in Miracles* (New York: Harper Collins, 1996), 190–91.

4. Danielle Kaeble and Mary Cowhig, "Correctional Populations in the United States, 2016," 1, accessed June 11, 2019, https://www.bjs.gov/content/pub/pdf/cpus16.pdf.

5. St. Benedict, Abbot of Monte Cassino, *St. Benedict's Rule*, trans. Patrick Barry, OSB (Mahwah, NJ: HiddenSpring, imprint of Paulist Press), 62.

# CHAPTER 3

||||||||||||||||||||||||||||||||||||||||||||||||||||||||||||

# The Church

## *Where Is It?*

## NOTES FROM THE MARGINS

I wrote earlier about how God, from a Christian perspective, has continually moved toward humanity from early recorded encounters in the stories of the Old Testament, to Jesus, whom we encounter as a person just like us, and to the Spirit of God, which is in every person. But if God wants to be so close to each of us that we can encounter him in one another, what does that mean for today's church? Doesn't that mean that the church needs to refocus a lot more on the human beings, each one individually, because that's exactly where God can be found?

Just like God's journey with human beings has changed and been renewed over the centuries, the path of the church also needs to be renewed over time. Time doesn't stand still. People and their needs change over the centuries, and the church needs to change too if it wants to implement what Jesus lived for us, being close to people so that people can be close to God.

Many people in the churches do feel that we need new paths, new ideas. No one has *the one* solution. Some want structural reforms, such as dropping the celibacy requirement for priests, ordaining women, allowing open participation in the selection of bishops, and so on. Others look for ways to deepen the faith. People often talk about a crisis of faith, not just personally, but globally. It sometimes seems to me that many people think, "If only the church would go 'back to its roots,' to the earlier form of Mass, saying the rosary, and increased prayer, everything would be all right again." We certainly need a deeper faith, but not a return to things that used to work but have stopped working. God is a God of journey, of setting out. Countless biblical stories in the Old and New Testaments show this. But I rarely hear people ask, For what purpose is God leading his church to and through changes? Where is the journey headed?

In the face of sinking membership in many churches, fewer congregants in services, and smaller and more distant parishes, there seems to be a decrease in faith that goes beyond denominations like Lutheran or Catholic. But I don't believe that this is a true decline of belief. I doubt that people have less faith, if faith is defined as the longing for a final answer, for something "more" in one's life. Instead, I think that people aren't finding satisfying answers in the way that most churches live and proclaim faith, or that churches are giving answers to questions people never asked.

If we find God primarily in the people around us, then hasn't the time come for the church to turn back to people, rather than sitting in empty rooms and waiting for people to come, or complaining that fewer people are taking on volunteer work in congregations? The question would then have to be, Where are people today? Where can I best encounter them and therefore God?

One of the reasons why it's so easy to feel the changes that have come over the church with Pope Francis is that his predecessor, Pope Benedict, was considered shier and more reticent. Where Benedict held his daily Mass in the company of his secretary and housekeepers, Francis moved among the people from his first day as pope. Instead of moving into the papal chambers, he kept his room in the Vatican guesthouse. Even today, that's where he celebrates Mass every day with guests. He eats with them, shows up unannounced in the Vatican cafeteria, and makes surprise visits to prisons, hospitals, and poor or violent housing projects. Early on, critics said that Francis was treating the divine office disrespectfully. The pope, they argued, is Christ's earthly representative, a divine authority in the world, and cannot simply go among the people. But in that sense, Francis was following directly in Jesus's footsteps.

Jesus did *nothing but* being among the people, particularly those on the margins! In other words, in the church, near God, there's room for everyone. In this sense, it's especially among people who don't feel they belong, who don't think they're pious enough, who feel small because they know so little about faith and God, that we find "other-spaces." They are other-spaces because the church needs to get its bearings here. It needs to reorient. What makes Jesus so fascinating is that he challenged people by talking about God in new and different ways, and by walking new paths. He went to all those who are left out by today's church or who feel the institution of the church has nothing for them. He went to the people who don't belong to any religion or faith to give their longing room. Jesus says the door will be opened for those who knock. Those who seek will find.

The way I see it, people can still be found where Jesus found them, and where Pope Francis is seeking them out today—on the margins. So, I would like to make a few "notes on the margins" below, pointing out places where people are waiting to be found, and explaining attitudes that can lead us back to encountering God in others.

# Journeying

God is a God of journeys, of setting out. I wrote earlier how Abraham was accompanied by God on his way, and how God showed himself to Abraham over and over again. It was the same with the people of Israel during their exodus from Egypt. For forty years, the Israelites journeyed through the desert accompanied by their God. This image of a people on a journey has shaped the church even into the present day. The church sees itself as a journeying community. We can see only the first inklings of the kingdom of God as Jesus proclaimed it. Building it, making it real on earth, requires work and dedication. Jesus, too, was always journeying, never staying in one place for too long. He wandered, went to the people, sought them out, visited, and walked with them. In a way, he brought God to them, carried him to them, making him visible and tangible for them. Jesus did not sit down in one place and wait for the people to come to him, listen to him, or adore him. When they came in large crowds, he hadn't "ordered them there" or announced his coming as any kind of event. Instead, his reputation preceded him. People came to him out of their own need, because they wanted to hear his message or hoped he would heal them, but he always first found them where they lived, wherever they dwelt with their questions, problems, and worries.

Many people in the church distinguish between contemplative and active faith, between the world and God. But God occurs in the midst of the world, in the midst of the people. God enters into the world, into people, through Jesus. In recent years, there has been a great deal of discussion in church circles that the church must and should "go there," that it can't wait for people to come to it, but instead needs to seek people out where they live, where they work, and where they ask about God, debate with him, find him, and let themselves be found.

When I was a child, it was normal for everyone to go to church on Sundays. There are many people who have that memory, because going to church was simply part of Sunday. Today, many churches lament the lack of practicing faithful, the lack of people who regularly visit the church. I too see more and more people go to church only occasionally and only occasionally make use of its services. I could complain; I could get angry; I could invoke the decline of Western civilization. Or I could see it as a chance to offer people a moment of meaning, a horizon of significance when they need it.

I'm always impressed that so many people, regardless of how they practice their faith themselves, bring their child for baptism. They seem to feel a great need to place this new life under the protection of a higher power and to ask for some sort of blessing for the child. This need might offer an opportunity for today's church to recognize that God has a message for his church: the church does reach people—if it chooses the right methods.

When today's bishops, however, keep repeating that we only need to deepen our faith, instead of making structural changes to the church, to me that feels like just parroting old ideas. The church's structures contribute to its credibility! Or fail to, if they seem outdated and rigid. Pope Francis keeps calling for courageous new suggestions for the future of the church, suggestions for how to help people discover God and God's footsteps within their horizons and for how to offer them new ways of seeing their life. The best biblical example of this type of attitude is the Apostle Paul. Newly arrived in Athens, he walks around and discovers that "the city was full of idols" (Acts 17:16).

Among the objects of worship, he finds an altar with the inscription, "To an unknown god" (Acts 17:23).

At the time, the Greeks were worried that they might have over-looked a god, and that this god might be angry and bring his wrath upon them. The Bible says that the Athenians always discussed ideas and were unusually eager to hear something new. Paul takes up the idea of the unknown God and surprises them by saying, "What therefore you worship as unknown, this I proclaim to you" (Acts 17:23).

Then he starts to talk about God and Jesus. He is standing before the Areopagus—an outcropping of rock outside the city, where ancient Greeks held court—not in a synagogue or a temple, but right out in the open and among the people. He talks about a God whom people suspect may exist but don't know. That's exactly how many people today feel. They sense that there's "something" there that goes beyond their life. They feel longing and are convinced that this longing is well-founded. Helping these people give their longing a name, to discover what they feel and are looking for—*that's* what church is! I believe that the Catholic Church needs to let go of the idea that its role is that of mediator, that priests have the job of bringing God's sacraments to earth. God is. God has always been. His very name is presence. Long before there were sacraments, God himself said, "Here I am." In the sacraments and liturgies, the point is to make God visible in signs, such as bread and wine. One could call it a "forensic" approach to God's presence among human beings, where the main focal point becomes journeying together with individual people and walking beside them however hard or beautiful the paths may be.

Some in the church hope that Francis will not be pope for too long, and that a truly "Catholic" pope will once again head the "Holy Roman Church." Personally, I'm convinced that after the style in which Francis has led the church, the new pope won't be able to go back. How anachronistic would it be if the next pope were to put on red shoes and set himself up as second to God! The Second Vatican Council, held from 1958 to 1963 and involving an assembly of all Catholic bishops, several theological advisers, and the pope, who all met with the goal of confronting the church with questions of the modern world, put it as follows in one of its statements: "The joys and the hopes, the griefs and the anxieties of the men of this age, especially those who are poor or in any way afflicted, these are the joys and hopes, the griefs and anxieties of the followers of Christ" (*Gaudium et spes* 1).[1]

This resonates with a new conception of what theological discourses call "Christian fellowship." Christians, and thus the church, are called to engage in fellowship with the people of today, to share their lives and be with them as Jesus was. Wherever people enter into conversation, share their joys, hopes, fears, and sadness—wherever a crack opens up and God shines through—that is where church happens, as a congregation and community of hoping, loving people.

In that case, however, church stops being only the visible community around a liturgical center. It's not just a congregation that gathers around the altar in its own building. It's also on the margins, and beyond compact congregations and official ecclesiastical roles, that Christianity happens. Today, we call this a "liquid church." That doesn't mean that the church is "superfluous," but it also doesn't mean the "evaporation of faith," as some said several years ago. When something evaporates, it's gone. When something becomes liquid, it changes its state. Those who, mostly in academic discussions, talk about a liquid church are making the assumption that young people today have lives that are "fluid." With more settled lives, most people fit in. But today's life circumstances and life plans, family models and partnership roles are more flexible and varied than ever, so too conceptions of Christian practice. This means that young people are no longer clear about what church means and what one has to do or not do. In the words of Professor Michael Schüßler, describing the liquid church, these conceptions have often become "mosaic pieces in the secular puzzle of daily cultural practice." In other words, people no longer have anything like the attachment to the church that they used to have, but religion, faith, and Christianity still occur in their lives, like different puzzle pieces in a mosaic. In some cases, these puzzle pieces are actually becoming more important. One can criticize or lament these developments, but that won't help.

In a book on change in religion, Rainer Bucher, an Austrian pastoral theologian, writes, "A Church which does not confront the 'world of its time,' a church which remains in only supposedly invulnerable spaces and certainties, does not do justice to its mission. In service of this mission it must dare to brave risk: its place is the open sea of devotion."[2]

If the church wants to be important to people today, it has to engage with the things that happen in the lives of those people. Just like people, it needs to accept the processes of change seen in the increasingly fluid lifestyles of social and societal existence. It can't try, in a reactionary and desperate way, to preserve things that can't be preserved anymore. Closing our eyes and denying what we dislike does not help. It might be that opening our eyes leads us to the exciting discovery that God is imminently present among and within the people of today.

# Monasteries

Many of these "modern" people, these seekers and questioners, may not find their way into churches, but we do encounter them in our abbey. Frequently, they are in a phase of personal change and upheaval, maybe a job crisis, a midlife crisis, or a failing marriage. Without even meaning to, often these changes also broach the subject of God. Many people feel something larger than themselves and wonder whether there is a meaning behind the fact that their life has taken this turn.

Many times, people today are seeking other-spaces outside their normal lives, places where they can look into themselves or gain perspective by drawing apart from their day-to-day life. People typically consider monasteries "spiritual" places, but to me, they are exactly this kind of other-space. There are many reasons for this. Many monasteries are relatively isolated, so they are already other-spaces, spaces on the border between civilization and nature, where one can forget the noise and bustle of a city and find some inner quiet. Also, the daily structure within monasteries makes them other-spaces from how most people experience their daily lives. Sure, many people have a kind of routine, which can be paralyzing as well. But because the monastery's schedule is structured around times of prayer, so that there are regular breaks in which to reflect and move from the "world out there" to one's inner world, this structure is experienced as healing rather than paralyzing. Not least, monasteries are other-spaces because they live by different values than most of the communities where people live today. Instead of aiming for "more, faster, better," monasteries tend to focus on less. Instead of consumerism and careers, monasteries emphasize balance and reduction to find one's own appropriate measure.

I recently led a course in our monastery, together with a sculptor. The topic was "simplicity." I was amazed and surprised at how the stone we were carving acted as a kind of role model. In order to find the form, to make it clearly recognizable, a stone mason or sculptor does nothing other than cut away stone. That is just what the people who come to our monastery want. They want to reach clarity in themselves, to find themselves and their true form, to work on and polish it, and to gain a clearer perspective on their life, and maybe on God as well.

The term *simplicity* also applies to our daily life as monks. We limit ourselves to one room to live in, don't accumulate many material possessions, don't practice a lavish lifestyle, reflect on truth in our regular prayers, and try to live a whole life simply, while finding inner richness and fullness. That's certainly one of the essential wishes that moves people to come to our monastery.

# Pilgrimages

Today, if we are looking for people filled with spiritual longing and a wish for a community in which they can find answers, we will probably find these people on one of the many paths of pilgrimage all over the world. After several decades in which people almost looked down on pilgrimages or saw them as something for only the most pious, this ancient religious practice has made an incredible comeback over the past fifteen years.

What's fascinating is that this tradition exists in almost all religions, not just in Christianity. It may be linked with a very deep, fundamental experience to which so many people are journeying. Today, not only faithful Christians travel along the Camino de Santiago, the pilgrimage to Compostela in Spain. Those who feel alienated by hierarchical church structure and the more traditional religious practices especially see these paths as an opportunity to experience the deeper meaning they seek in their lives.

Pilgrimage causes people to concentrate on the essentials, such as a backpack with necessaries. Simplicity plays a big part here, and it can be amazing how little you really need on the road. Simplicity is mirrored in the daily routine of getting up, washing, eating breakfast, packing the backpack, putting on shoes, walking, arriving, resting, and sleeping. Many people discover that this reduction, this feeling of not needing to rethink everything all the time, of not being constantly faced with new decisions but living each day in a pattern, that this experience can make them very happy.

Pilgrimages take loads off our backs, the load of the daily slog at home and stresses at work. They give us free space. When we walk, we pass on our loads to the ground, via our feet. When we walk, we get moving, outside in the world and inside ourselves.

The most important aspect, however, is the companions we meet along the way. Etymologically, a companion is a person who shares their bread with me (from the Latin *cum pane*, meaning "with bread"). In other words, this is a person who is by my side for a time, who maybe shares something vital with me. This strengthens and encourages me.

If the church wants to follow the path of Jesus and walk toward people, then roads of pilgrimage would be one place where people can be found. Everyone on the road is carrying their own baggage and has their own reason for having set out, their own reason for breaking out of their "old" or regular life. Churches here could be stops on the side of the road, inviting people to rest if they need and offering a safe space where there is spiritual sustenance as well. Just like Jesus, the churches could ask, "What do you want me to do for you?" Or, in a more modern way: What can I do for you? How can I help you find something that will soothe the longing of your heart?

# Hospitality

It's no secret that many things will change in the church over the coming decades. In Germany, for example, parishes are increasingly grouped together, and in the United States, there is a similar trend of decreasing individual parishes. But canon law dictates that only priests can head congregations, so the lack of priests will make the problem worse in the long run. Add to that the fact that many people find that church services aren't lively, but dead collections of phrases, some in a language that most don't understand. Even faithful Christians often have difficulty explaining what the liturgy actually means.

That's why many people are looking for alternative places where they can feel that the things that are preached and said come "from real life," that people are living what they pray and preach. That is certainly a reason why people come to monasteries.

St. Benedict put hospitality into the *Rule* he wrote for his monks. He even says exactly what I tried to show above: the monks should see Christ in every guest and invite in God in every person seeking entry. Benedictine hospitality has now actually become proverbial! What fascinated me about my monastery of Münsterschwarzach was its openness.

Anyone can come as they are and go as they are as well. No one tries to proselytize or preach morality to "improve" the people who come through our gates. That is true for our youth work, just as much as for how we receive visitors in the guesthouse or the *Recollectio*-House.

In our monastery, we hold a service each morning in our crypt. Each confrere presides over this service for a week. Whenever it's my turn, I follow the example of one of my older confreres in asking all the guests attending the service (sometimes only ten, sometimes up to forty) to gather in a circle around the altar for the Lord's Prayer. I know some of the guests from conversations, others I have never seen before. But each of them stands there with their story, in their own situation, this morning around the altar. Together, we pray and then celebrate the Eucharist. I'm always touched that people thank us for this. They feel invited in, accepted, valued. No one has to stay where they are, perhaps feeling bad for not being particularly "holy" this morning, because their life isn't in good shape and they don't know whether God still loves them. It's a single moment of encounter, and everyone goes out into their day after the service. But they know this: I'm allowed to be here, I get to participate in this life here, even if just for a little bit. Here are people who see themselves in this moment and don't ask whether they're "allowed" or not, but just enjoy this short communion through meal and prayer.

We should see the celebration of the Mass in this context, too. About ten years ago, when Pope Benedict XVI allowed the Tridentine Mass (the form of the Mass that is read in Latin, facing away from the congregation) as an "extraordinary form" of the Catholic service, half the people was overjoyed, and the other half was outraged. The joy came from those who had always seen the Tridentine Mass as the only true celebration of the Catholic faith, and who saw today's form as too much "freestyle" and "improv," with too many words and too little prayerful silence. These are the same people who attack Pope Francis now. When Benedict was criticized, they called for loyalty to the pope, and now refuse to offer exactly that. I get the sense that this is a particular vision of the church, as keeper of the true, unchangeable teachings, as the guarantor of truth, a rock in modern times and modern thinking, which are supposed to be ungodly in and of themselves.

But the Tridentine Mass originated in a particular time as well, and so did church teaching. They did not fall from heaven ready-made. The disciples, apostles, and early Christians all grappled with and argued over what actually is and isn't Christian. I remember how, in my religion class in high school, we read a passage by Johann Baptist Metz, one of the founders of Liberation Theology. He had written a text for the Würzburg Synod, the council of clergy that met in the 1970s to discuss what the revisions of the Second Vatican Council might mean for the German church. Metz wrote that "the Kingdom of God is not indifferent to fair trade practices."

I wrote an entire essay on this sentence. He was trying to say nothing less than that the kingdom of God was not a refuge to hide in, but rather occurred among us in the real world. It happened in the markets and in economics. Moving the altar—the symbol of God's presence—after the Second Vatican Council, makes this clear. It was now supposed to be close to the people of God, not a distant place where an inaccessible priest performed the Mass with his back to the faithful. The priest was supposed to stand among the people. This showed that the real concern was the people who congregated in the name of Christ, the seeking and questioning faithful with whom God was wandering.

Even if the advocates of the Tridentine Mass may dispute this, I see a clear difference between the two forms of the Mass. The Tridentine Mass offers God a sacrifice, the sacrifice of Christ on the cross, which we relive in the Mass, because it unites God with his people. The Mass celebrated by the congregation gathered around an altar signifies that we are celebrating a meal together. It's a feast of love, where Jesus in love is giving himself to those he loves. He is giving himself to us. The introduction of the Mass in local languages finally enabled the faithful to actually understand what the priest is saying. I often think that Jesus spoke in such a way that people understood what he was saying. Why should the Mass be any different? I believe that the church doesn't need to defend God or fearfully preserve tradition. It does not need to shrink back, away from the people, into a form that God never conceived or intended. God can protect himself. But the Christian message has to be that God is right here with us, among us, and present in this world through the people of the world.

The same is true for people who complain that today's faithful only expect an occasional service from the church or participate in the congregation only once in a while, but otherwise don't show up and aren't even willing to take on volunteer positions and support the community. We just must accept that people today go to church only occasionally. It's more important to think about what kind of support or inspiration we can offer them in this hour, in their situation, whatever that may be. I sometimes think that Jesus, too, met people only occasionally. Many of the people he healed or encountered in the villages he walked through never saw him again, and yet the encounter changed their life.

That would also mean that the structure of the church needs to change from the bottom up, because it's still based on regular attendance, on community life with services for people who are there year-round, for every occasion, whether personal or ecclesiastical. But can we imagine a church that follows Jesus's example and offers help to people when they need it? Many rigid, outdated, and empty practices would fall away, and that might make the church's message more relevant to people.

I remember how, during my time as religion teacher at a small high school, I was preparing a group of students for their confirmation. It was a small group and we were selecting the readings for the confirmation service together. One student suggested, and the others approved, that we read the gospel passage in which Jesus calms the storm. I asked him why he chose this story in particular. "It's obvious," he answered. "You can't keep God down." I was so impressed by his answer that I told him, "If you can remember that for the rest of your life, you'll know everything you ever need to know." It was a tiny moment, but filled, at least in my experience, with deep meaning.

# Rituals

Let's get back to the people who bring their child for baptism, or want God's blessing on their marriage, or a church burial for their relatives, even though they aren't otherwise active in church life. Some are already cynically referring to first communion as the "last communion," because barely a month later, most of the children no longer go to church. There are also of course those who go to church only on Christmas or Easter. Others come to us in the abbey to have their child baptized, because the local priest or minister refuses, with the justification that the parents are unmarried or never come to church.

I always wonder, "What longing leads these people to us, to the church, to a service? Is it really just habit, the way it's always been or how their family has always done it? And how can I talk with these people in such a way that they understand the message? What's the most important message that I can give them for their journey?"

People who have stopped trusting the church are turning to independent consultants and ritual-makers instead. What's interesting is that in that business, there are a lot of former priests. Instead of a minister, an emcee or other speaker shapes some ritual at the beginning of life, at a wedding, or at the end of life. People have always looked for divine protection or blessing for the big changes in their life. Clearly, we have some archaic longing for blessing and protection. Everywhere in nature, there are cycles of becoming, growing, maturing, wilting, dying, and being reborn. Why should we be the exception to these cycles, and why shouldn't we look for blessing at these critical points in life?

Christians view these rituals with anger or hatred as being un-Christian or "New Age." But they express a question, and even a question of God to his church and to the people who make up his church. Some even say that the decline of the church has a divine purpose, which is that everyone should see: We can't keep going like this. Something has to change.

But how should we keep going? What might change look like? The fact that people long for rituals, that they invite and pay people to create independent rituals, shows that they haven't lost the desire for ritual. They aren't "godless" in the way some faithful like to complain. Actually, it's exactly the opposite. They are looking for a blessing, a protection, or a foothold that they can't find in their secular lives, that a secular life can't give them. They are alienated from the ways churches today act. When I prepare people for a church ritual, I find that more of them are expressing personal wishes. For example, they may want to sing particular songs that mean a lot to them or that express what the ritual means to them. Or in weddings they may want to exchange vows they wrote themselves, in addition to the vows that the church mandates. People are trying to shape rituals at important moments in their lives so that the rituals reflect their lives, and they see the church as inflexible in its rituals and traditions, if not downright dogmatic. This begs the question of whether, or how much, the church—with its liturgy, services, and rituals—touches people in the lives they are living. Or is it instead upholding and passing on formulas that to many people are empty and meaningless? Does the church long to return to people, to take up their language and understanding?

For example, on the evening of October 31, many people celebrate Halloween, which some see as an esoteric, commercial holiday that has completely eclipsed All Saints' Day on November 1. But the name Halloween actually means "Hallows'-eve," or "evening before All Saints' (Hallows') Day"! This is the day on which the church remembers all saints, particularly those who don't have their own feast day during the year. The church is trying to make sure that no one is left out. The roots of Halloween come from a pagan Celtic celebration connected with certain rituals, celebrated around the beginning of November to mark the end of summer, the "bright" time of year. At the same time, pagans believed that with the beginning of winter, the dark powers grew in strength and the dead could return. The rites were meant to combat this darkness and to emphasize the light, which shone into people's lives through the saints.

Today, kids go from house to house in costumes, asking for candy. There are parties with spooky costumes, maybe in order to make the dark and the dead less frightening by bringing them "into the light." I see this as a way of dealing with the coming darkness, which one feels clearly around that time because summertime ends, and it starts to get dark early.

People are looking for new rituals because the old ones no longer mean anything to them, or because they don't understand them. But the church with its old rituals is not trying to do anything different than the people of today with their new rituals. On All Saints' Day, the church celebrates all those saints who are by God's side, living in the light. This expresses the hope that the people living in the world are not left to the darkness and the dark powers. I see those two ideas as expressing the same need, the same longing. Maybe the right question to ask is what a celebration of All Saints' Day would need to look like in order to take on the beginning of seasons with long, dark nights and do justice to people's needs today.

Actually, that is something that the church itself has always done. During Christianity's early days, it incorporated so-called pagan rites that were part of people's lives, reinterpreting them and filling them with Christian meaning. Christmas, for example, goes back to the festival of a Roman sun god. The church was pointing out that the true sun, the actual light of the world, is the Christian God, who became man in Jesus Christ on Christmas Day.

God became man to encounter people "eye-to-eye," on their

level. He does not want to remain the "great unknown" but reveals himself, tangibly and imminently to people in their language and their way of life. In the end, rituals are supposed to help us feel God, not as some force that reigns far off in the world, but as someone who, in the important moments of our life, protects, blesses, and walks with us. This means that, just as in Jesus's time, the form and language of today's rituals need to enable us to feel, accept, and understand God's message.

*Of course* this can mean questioning previous rituals, rites, and liturgies. We may even need new forms that we haven't found yet. But the question is the same: Does the church want to preserve all its forms and traditions, or does it want to encounter others and live in emulation of Christ?

## Embracing a Modern Zeitgeist

Again and again, I read that the church needs to be an antidote to the modern zeitgeist. What this usually means is that the spirit of modernity is equated with individualism, and the writer is complaining that everyone more or less lives however they want to, including putting together their own religion in the way they like.

When I read these thoughts, I notice myself tense up. To me, it's just too negative a way of thinking! It's too simple as well. The church is always the church of its own time. God's Spirit blows where it will. Whatever we today feel is an unquestionable dogma grew out of the needs of a particular age and was based on a particular worldview. In its teaching, the Catholic Church recognizes different "degrees of truth," meaning that not all church teachings are irrevocably set in stone. In its early days, Christianity was something radically new, part of its own zeitgeist. It was completely blasphemous in the eyes of Jewish theologians, something that could not possibly come from God. Jesus, being so close to outcasts and pariahs from Jewish law, could not be sent by God, much less be the Messiah or Savior! But Jesus—and the developing faith of Christianity—did not shy away from setting out and approaching people. Already in those days, the disciples went to the ends of the world, proclaiming the new and responding to the questions, worries, and needs of those they encountered. When the disciples received the Spirit of Christ, they set out away from synagogues and temples and toward the people. They visited them in their homes, healed them, strengthened them, and led them out of their suffering and misery. They did all of it in a language the people immediately understood. God's Spirit always works in the here and now. That's why what was important then is important now: responding to people in the places and ways they live and exist today, answering their suffering, and affirming the ways they are looking for God. We need to give answers to their questions that are supportive and respond to their longing. This is exactly what the Second Vatican Council, in fact, called "aggiornamento," meaning "modernization" or "bringing up-to-date." The church is challenged to answer the times in which it lives.

I was shocked when I witnessed a recent discussion on how we should view theological research. Many voices were arguing that theological research was subject to the magisterium, just like everything else. In the end, this means that the Catholic Church decides whether the results of scholarship and research are wrong or right, or whether they are "allowed." But research has to be independent; otherwise, it's just lobbying or propaganda. I could sense that there was fear of the results of today's research, which might go against previous doctrine. If that happens, the church needs to face up to it. When a significant number of theologians say that there is no theological ground for refusing women's ordination, or when researchers consistently say that homosexuality is not a disease but a natural tendency, just like heterosexuality, or when we find people who feel themselves in the wrong body and cannot be strictly assigned as male or female, the church needs to engage with these facts.

When, in one German diocese, ten thousand signatures are collected for the *viri probati*—men who are married but have proved themselves in the Christian faith, and whose ordination is often called for as a step for progress—and the local bishop refuses to go into the question at all, I wonder, "How seriously are we taking the lay men and women who are called to be prophets?" Every baptized child is a prophet of God. That is another rediscovery of the Second Vatican Council, and it needs to be our first emphasis today.

Pope Francis has frequently called for courageous suggestions for the future of the church, but where are these suggestions? Who says that he would refuse if, say, a German bishop or the Conference of German Bishops made him some courageous suggestions? And why do we need to solve all questions on the level of the global church? If there are urgent questions in Europe and the West that are not urgent in Africa, for example, regional churches can find regional answers. Of course, we need criteria for recognizing the Spirit of God. But so often, being against change is just too negative, too easy. The Second Vatican Council offered useful approaches for understanding the spirituality of the church. Couldn't individualism and so-called DIY religion be part of this spiritual movement, a movement of our time in which we can find the Spirit of God? One of the criticisms of these new spiritualities is often that Christianity is not a "wellness religion," meaning a religion that an individual organizes for themselves until it is no longer challenging but comfortable. The criticism is that faith is not just about feeling good. It's true that Christianity challenges us and can cost lives. But if Christian spirituality can talk about the *dulcedo dei*, the sweetness of God, or if Jesus invites us to find peace and strength in him and even calls God "Father," then surely feeling good can be an important part, and longing for this kind of comfort can be seen as a longing for God.

For far too long, Christianity has had a reputation for asceticism and denial, for believing that "faith should not be fun or spark joy." But how much joy can arise in us when we feel God's strength within us, when we feel God empowering us to be ourselves, or to stand up and preach! This is how the prophet Miriam must have felt, singing of the Lord as liberator, after he led the Israelites through the Red Sea. God is a liberator. It is also ours to feel and "taste" that truth. Faith is not just "believing something to be true" or "assenting to doctrines" or even "a religion of the mind." If the center is a meal, a taste of bread and wine, then becoming one with God, and sensual experience, joy and enjoyment are just as important.

I like to quote a sentence that I read several years ago and that has been with me ever since: "Entrust yesterday to the mercy of God; leave tomorrow to God's providence; but live today, for God embraces the world through you." We can find God only in this world, in our lives here, in the time and place in which we live. We find God in this reality, just as it is, not in a reality that one or another person might like to have. The church is not what it once was. There may be people who think that "the Church has survived worse; let's wait and see. It will make it through these times as well." But it would be sad if "surviving" was the goal, rather than spreading the good news. It's my impression that there is a thin line between spreading the message of God and narcissism on the part of those doing the spreading. I often feel that individual clergy are more concerned with their own splendor, with making sure they have an exalted position, a special calling, a place as a defender of right teachings and the church. This was just what Jesus was preaching against, against those who sit in the front row, who focus on their fancy clothing and want to be seen.

Once again, I'm convinced that Christians don't need to defend or assert anything. We need to *be* something. We need open spaces for God's presence in the midst of the world, in this reality and present time. For those in the church, that needs to beg the question: Where does God want to lead his people? What new impulses might lie in the world other than to condemn it?

# Compassion

I think that today's church has a lot of trouble with unconditional acceptance of human beings in the way Jesus modeled it. For example, no papal document in recent memory has caused as much uproar as the encyclical *Amoris laetitia*.[3] It's mostly about pastoral care for married couples and families, but the attention focused on whether the pope would allow remarried divorcees to receive communion. In a footnote, the pope wrote that "in certain cases," those faithful can have "the aid of the sacraments." This set off a discussion about what the note meant. The German Conference of Bishops emphasized that divorcees must have support and pastoral care, as well as consideration on a case-by-case basis. Then, after discussing the situation with their priest, they could come to a point in their own conscience that they deserved to receive communion. If, on the one hand, divorcees and remarried faithful hear that they are an important part of the church and still members, but on the other hand, are denied communion, many people think that the church loses credibility.

A few bishops then point to "spiritual communion." Although some people receive communion in bread and wine, those who "aren't allowed" can still receive Jesus spiritually. I'm not sure anyone really understands what that means, or what the point is. God is a living God. He became flesh and wants to communicate himself sensually to us, in bread and wine. So often, I see how liberating it can be for people to find spaces where they can just be who they are. Like for Zacchaeus. By inviting himself over, Jesus opened up a space for change. Accepting Zacchaeus was the first and most important step. Jesus didn't say, "Go home and give away your fortune, and when you've paid everything back, I'll come visit you." He said, "I must dine with you," just like that. He set no conditions. That's why we need a church that will act in the same way, including by using language that heals, signals inclusion, and offers understanding. We need spaces and language that lets people feel this truth: God heals. This reminds me of another exciting sentiment of Pope Francis, that communion isn't for saints, but is there to give the weak strength.

In fact, if Francis's papacy had a motto, it could be "Compassion." Francis wants to approach people, and to raise up and strengthen every person, just like Jesus did, and just like Jesus says of God. More than once, Pope Francis has made clear that even as a pope, he doesn't have to decide matters of Catholic teaching. The individual's conscience and their own responsibility in faith are still above the teaching of the magisterium of the church. It's also true that the law was made for man, not man for the law. In the end, the law is love, which turns with compassion to those in need.

Jesus always accepted people however they and their situation happened to be. He showed them love and closeness. In my work as an emergency counselor, I see how important it is to just be there, to accept, and to go with people instead of judging or condemning them. Many victims of trauma or grief ask about God, or ask, "Why?" Why did God allow this to happen? It often takes a long time for these people to accept the situation as it is. It can happen that, after years of dealing with the situation, they still don't have an answer for this "Why?" but nevertheless feel God supporting them in the situation, right there with them in their lives.

Someone once said that it's important to stand by your imperfections. Not everything has to be perfect in front of or for God. We're allowed to have gaps, painful situations, detours, and wrong turns. Jesus most of all showed, in his parables and his encounters with people on the margins, that he heals and turns compassionately to the broken, the hurt, the sick, and the misled. In our *Recollectio*-House, we sometimes host a workshop in which guests can make art with shards. They take broken glass, clay shards of pots, china, or splinters, and turn them into something new. They make works of art that look whole and completely unbroken. There is deep symbolism in that: Wherever people at first see only something broken and fragmentary, God can see the possibility of a new future, of resurrection.

# INSTEAD OF A CONCLUSION

At the end of this book, I want to return, in a way, to how I started: with the people in the Bible who are found by God. One of them, whom I've already mentioned, is the prophet Elijah. Here is a story of a person who reaches the end of his strength and is then found by God. To Elijah, God turns out to be completely different than he had thought up until that point. My thoughts on Elijah's story and personality will round out this book by summing up what has been important to me. The text I am referring to is in the Old Testament and is quoted below.

I hope you will have an exciting journey of discovering God in the countless situations in your life, of letting yourself be discovered by and surprised by God.

> At that place [Mount Horeb] he [Elijah] came to a cave and spent the night there....
> [The Lord] said, "Go out and stand on the mountain before the LORD, for the LORD is about to pass by." Now there was a great wind, so strong that it was splitting mountains and breaking rocks in pieces before the LORD, but the LORD was not in the wind; and after the wind an earthquake, but the LORD was not in the earthquake; and after the earthquake a fire, but the LORD was not in the fire; and after the fire a sound of sheer silence. When Elijah heard it, he wrapped his face in his mantle and went out and stood at the entrance of the cave. (1 Kgs 19:9–13)

At a Sunday service about ten years ago, a confrere of mine preached on the prophet Elijah, including the two passages given here and previously in the book. In his sermon, this confrere said a sentence that I have not forgotten to this day: "God is not in the things that cause fear."

On Mount Horeb, Elijah experiences earthquakes, storms, and fire in all their destructive, terrifying power. In them, the story says, God is not. Elijah has just won a "test of the gods," and the angry and vengeful losing side, the priests of Baal and their queen Jezebel, have pursued Elijah to the brink of exhaustion. He knows that his life is in

94

danger of being swallowed up by the eager fire he has ignited in his challenge to Baal. He has taken a big risk, putting fear into others and winning in the end, and now he sees this triumphant behavior come back to haunt him.

Until recently, the church kept going through similar scenes of seeking to prove the power of God, many priests stoked the flames of hell and invoked purgatory. They may have had the good intentions of moving people to faith and repentance, even of saving souls. But what they caused was fear, and that fear came back to haunt the church, because people are now turning away, with their souls more hurt than healed. Elijah is going through something like the people who have inwardly turned away from the church. He flees into the desert, exhausted and spent. There, he sits in a deep depression, hiding beneath a bush and hoping to die. He falls back in on himself, feeling hurt and resentful. With those thoughts, he falls asleep.

When he wakes up at the touch of an angel, he finds water and bread "baked on hot stones," as the Bible says. This food was baked on the warm remains of the fire he lit. But Elijah falls back asleep, so the angel wakes him a second time and tells him to eat. He eats the bread baked on hot stones. It's almost as if Elijah was meant to feel, to experience and finally understand what fire is actually for: to feed people. This is what God is like. He comes in the form of an angel and strengthens Elijah. God doesn't retaliate or avenge himself. He just leads Elijah by a gentle touch until Elijah can understand who and how God is. Maybe that's exactly why Yahweh agreed to be tested against Baal, so that Elijah could learn and understand God, so that he could see the difference and feel who God really is, and see that he has used God to play himself up as the big divine warrior and hero for God. Today's divine warriors also set fires, destroy, and terrorize people. Elijah learns that that is the exact opposite of God's way!

When Elijah comes up Mount Horeb, tired from fleeing, he goes into a cave. That is the image of the womb. Elijah is protecting himself but is also regressing, is pulling back from reality, just as adults sometimes do by falling back into childish ways of acting in order to try to get out of conflicts and challenges. This kind of retreat is a little like pulling the blanket over one's own head. Elijah needs this retreat into the cave of depression, resentment, and hurt at the whole situation.

I know those feelings from my own experience. Sensing the need for growth, we go back a step, maybe to gather our strength or to take a run-up to a new challenge. In his retreat into this cave, Elijah witnesses the primal forces that can terrify us: fire, storm, and earthquake. But after the powerful, terrifying forces have moved on, Elijah steps out of the cave, out of his depression and fear. He stands tall and wraps his face in his mantle. This is the cloak of God, the mantle of the prophet, which he will later pass on to Elisha and which Elisha will recognize as a call to prophecy. Elijah cloaks his eyes, meaning he recognizes in a new way his call to prophecy, to speak of God. He finds God in the sound of pure silence, but this isn't just quiet. It is an uplifting silence, something that requires great mindfulness to be perceived at all.

God's presence, God's silent sound, God's uplifting quiet, in which everything is cloaked, can often get lost in the fire and eagerness of those who see today's debates (refugees, transgender rights, marriage equality) as the downfall of the Christian West. Fear consumes them, and they see only the negative. They retreat into the church as if it were a castle under siege, the same church that once vocally and terrifyingly proclaimed the omnipotence of God in a doctrine set in stone.

As Christians today, however, we are called to come out of this cave, to go "to the margins" and bring people nourishing bread and refreshing water, to discover God's outstretched hand together, his uplifting presence, his hope and love that can heal the wounds of their lives.

All Christians are prophets; all Christians are cloaked in the mantle of prophecy. We are all enveloped, surrounded, and protected by a strengthening, uplifting, hopeful, nourishing, life-giving, and trust-building presence. I can feel and sense it, but only if I take a step back from fiery eagerness that can destroy and from disappointment in the supposedly bad, anti-Christian, anti-religious world. I need to take a step back from the things that cause fear or want to terrify, even in the church. God is not in things that cause fear.

# Notes

1. Pope Paul VI, *Pastoral constitution on the Church in the modern world: Gaudium et spes* (December 7, 1965), Papal Archive, The Holy See, http://www.vatican.va/archive/hist_councils/ii_vatican _council/documents/vat-ii_const_19651207_gaudium-et-spes_en .html.

2. Rainer Bucher, *…wenn nichts bleibt, wie es war: Zur prekären Zukunft der katholischen Kirche* [...when nothing remains as it once was: On the Catholic Church's precarious future] (Würzburg: Echter Verlag, 2017), 60.

3. Pope Francis, *Amoris laetitia* (March 19, 2016), Vatican Press, http://w2.vatican.va/content/dam/francesco/pdf/apost_exhortations/ documents/papa-francesco_esortazione-ap_20160319_amoris-laetitia _en.pdf.